The Redeemed Captive, Returning to ZION.

A Faithful HISTORY OF Remarkable Occurrences, IN THE Captivity AND THE Deliverance OF Mr. John Williams;

Minister of the Gospel, in DEERFIELD, Who, in the Desolation which befel that Plantation, by an Incursion of the French & Indians, was by them carried away, with his Family, and his Neighbourhood, unto CANADA.

Whereto there is annexed a SERMON Preached by him, upon his RETURN, at the Lecture in Boston, Decemb. 5 1706. On those Words, Luk. 8. 39. Return to thine own House, and shew how great Things God hath done unto thee.

Boston in N.E. Printed by B. Green, for Samuel Phillips, at the Brick Shop. 1707.

Printing Statement:

Due to the very old age and scarcity of this book, many of the pages may be hard to read due to the blurring of the original text, possible missing pages, missing text and other issues beyond our control.

Because this is such an important and rare work, we believe it is best to reproduce this book regardless of its original condition.

Thank you for your understanding.

The DEDICATION.

To His EXCELLENCY,

JOSEPH DUDLEY, Esqr.

Captain General and GOVERNOUR in Chief, in and over Her Majesties Province of the Massachusetts-Bay in New-England, &c.

SIR,

IT was a Satyrical Answer, and deeply reproachful to Mankind, which the Philosopher gave to that Question, *What soonest grows old?* Replyed, *Thanks.* The reproach of it would not be so sensible, were there not sensible Demonstrations of the Truth of it, in those that wear the Character of the Ingenuous. Such as are at first Surprized at, and seem to have no common relish of Divine Goodness ; yet too soon lose the Impression : *They Sang God's Praise, but soon forgat His Works.* That it should be thus with respect to our *Benefactors* on Earth, is contrary to the Ingenuity of Humane Nature : But that

our

our grateful Refentments of the Signal Favours of Heaven, fhould foon be worn off by Time, is to the laft degree Criminal and Unpardonable.

It would be unaccountable Stupidity in me, not to maintain the moft Lively and Awful Senfe of Divine Rebukes, which the Holy GOD has feen meet in Spotlefs Sovereignty to difpenfe to me, my Family and People, in delivering us into the hands of thofe that Hated us : who Led us into a ftrange Land ; *My Soul has Thofe ftill in Remembrance, and is Humbled in me* : However GOD has given us plentiful occafion to fing of Mercy as well as Judgment. The wonders of Divine Mercy, which we have feen in the Land of our Captivity, and Deliverance therefrom, cannot be forgotten without incurring the guilt of the Blackeft Ingratitude.

To preferve the Memory of *Thofe*, it has been thought adviſeable to Publiſh a Short Account of fome of *Thofe* Signal Appearances of Divine Power and Goodnefs for us ; hoping it may Serve to excite the *Praife, Faith* and *Hope* of all that Love GOD ; And may peculiarly Serve to Cheriſh a *Grateful Spirit*, and to render the Impreffions of GOD'S Mighty Works indelible on my Heart, and on

Thofe

The DEDICATION.

Those that with me, have feen the Wonders of the Lord, and Tafted of His Salvation : That we may not fall under that heavy Charge made againft *Ifrael* of old, Pfal. 78. 11, 42. *They forgat His works, and the wonders He fhewed them : They remembred not His Hand, nor the Day that He delivered them from the Enemy.*

And I cannot *SIR*, but think it moft agreeable to my Duty to GOD our Supream Redeemer, to mention your *EXCELLENCY'S* Name with Honour ; Since Heaven has Honoured you as the prime Inftrument in returning our Captivity. Sure I am, The Laws of Juftice and Gratitude (which are the Laws of God) do challenge from us the moft Publick acknowledgments of your uncommon Sympathy with us, your Children, in our bonds, Expreffed in all Endearing methods of Parental Care and Tendernefs. All your People are cherifht under your Wings, happy in your Goverment ; and are obliged to Blefs GOD for you : And among your People, thofe that are immediately expofed to the Outrages of the Enemy, have peculiarly felt Refrefhment from the benign Influences of your Wife and Tender Conduct ; and are under the moft Senfible engagements to acknowledge your EXCELLENCY. under GOD, as the breath of their Noftrils.

A 2   Your

The DEDICATION.

Your Uncommon Sagacity and Prudence, in contriving to loose the Bonds of your Captived Children; your unwearied Vigour, and Application, in pursuing them, to work our Deliverance, can never be enough Praised. It is most Notorious that nothing was thought too Difficult by you to Effect this Design; in that you readily sent your own Son, Mr. *William Dudley*, to undergo the hazards & hardships of a Tedious Voyage, that this affair might be Transacted with Success; which must not be forgotten, as an Expression of your great Solicitude & Zeal to recover us from the Tyranny & Oppression of our Captivity.

I doubt not but that the G O D, whom herein you have Served, will remember, and gloriously Reward you; And may Heaven long preserve you at our Helm, a Blessing so necessary for the Tranquility of this Province, in this Dark and Tempestuous Season; May the best of Blessings from the Father of Lights, be showred down upon your Person, Family & Government; which shall be the Prayer of,

Your EXCELLENCY'S
Most Humble, Obedient,
and Dutiful Servant,

John Williams.

THE
Redeemed Captive, Returning
TO
ZION.

THE History I am going to Write, proves, That Days of *Fasting* & *Prayer* without REFORMATION, will not avail, to Turn away the Anger of God from a Professing People ; & yet Witnesseth, How very advantagious, gracious Supplications are, to prepare particular Christians, Patiently to suffer the Will of God, in very trying Publick Calamities. For some of us moved with fear, set apart, a day of *Prayer*, to ask of God, either to spare, and save us from the hands of our Enemies, or to prepare us to Sanctify, and Honour Him in what way soever, He should come forth, towards us. The Places of Scripture from whence we were entertained, were *Gen.* 32. 10, 11. *I am not worthy of the least of all the Mercies, and of all the Truth which thou hast shewed unto thy servant : --- Deliver me, I pray thee*

A 4

thee, from the hand of my Brother, from the hand of Esau: for I fear him, lest he will come and smite me, and the Mother with the Children. [In the forenoon.] And *Gen. 32. 26. And he said, Let me go, for the day breaketh: and he said, I will not let thee go, except thou bless me.* [In the afternoon.] From which we were call'd upon to spread the causes of fear, relating to our own Selves, or Families before God; as also, how it becomes us with an undeniable importunity to be following God, with earnest Prayers for His blessing, in every condition. And it is very Observable, how *GOD* ordered our Prayers, in a peculiar manner to be going up to Him; to prepare us with a right *Christian Spirit*, to undergo, and endure Suffering Trials.

Not long after, the Holy, and Righteous God, brought us under great Trials, as to our Persons and Families, which put us under a necessity, of spreading before Him in a Wilderness, the distressing dangers and calamities of our Relations; Yea, that call'd on us notwithstanding seeming present frowns, to resolve by His Grace not to be sent away without a blessing. *Jacob* in wrestling has the hollow of his Thigh put out of joint; and it is said to him, *Let me go:* yet he is rather animated, to an Heroical Christian resolution to continue earnest, for the blessing, than discouraged from asking.

ON the Twenty-ninth of *February* 1703, 4. Not long before break of day, the Enemy came in like a Flood upon us; our Watch being unfaithful: an evil, whose awful effects, in a surprizal

rizal of our Fort, should befpeak all Watchmen to avoid, as they would not bring the charge of blood upon themfelves. They came to my Houfe in the beginning of the Onfet, and by their violent endeavours to break open Doors, and Windows, with *Axes*, and *Hatchets*, Awaken'd me out of Sleep ; on which I leapt out of bed, and running toward the door, perceived the Enemy making their entrance into the Houfe : I called to awaken two Souldiers, in the Chamber ; and returned towards my bed-fide, for my Arms : the Enemy immediately brake into the Room, I judge to the number of Twenty, with *Painted Faces*, and hideous Acclamations. I reach'd up my hands to the Bed-tefter, for my Piftol, uttering a fhort Petition to God, *For Everlafting Mercies for me & mine, on the account of the Merits of our Glorify'd Redeemer* ; Expecting a prefent paffage through the Valley of the fhadow of Death : Saying in my felf, as Ifaiah 38. 10, 11. *I faid, in the cutting off my days, I fhall go to the gates of the grave : I am deprived of the refidue of my years. I faid, I fhall not fee the Lord, even the Lord, in the land of the Living : I fhall behold man no more with the inhabitants of the World.* Taking down my Piftol, I Cockt it, and put it to the breaft of the firft Indian who came up ; but my Piftol miffing fire, I was feized by Three Indians, who difarmed me, and bound me Naked, as I was in my Shirt, and fo I ftood for near the fpace of an hour : binding me, they told me they would carry me to Quebeck. My Piftol miffing fire, was an occafion of my Life's being preferved : Since which I have alfo found it profitable to be crofs'd in my own
Will.

VIII. The judgment of God did not long slumbe[r]
against one of the Three which took me, who wa[s]
a Captain, for by Sun-rising he received a Mort[al]
Shot, from my next Neighbours house ; who oppo[s-]
sed so great a number of *French* & *Indians* as Thre[e]
hundred, and yet were no more than Seven me[n]
in an Ungarison'd house.

I cannot relate the distressing care I had fo[r]
my dear Wife, who had lien-In but a few Wee[ks]
before, and for my poor Children, Family, an[d]
Christian Neighbours. The Enemy fell to rifflin[g]
the house, and entred in great numbers into ever[y]
room of the house. I beg'd of God, to Remembe[r]
Mercy in the midst of Judgment : that He would [so]
far restain their Wrath, as to prevent their Mu[r-]
dering of us : that we might have *Grace to Glorif[y]
His Name, whether in Life or Death* ; and as I wa[s]
able committed our State to God. The Enemi[es]
who entred the House were all of them *Indians* an[d]
Maqua's, insulted over me a while, holding up Hat[ch-]
chets over my head, threatning to burn all I had[,]
but yet God beyond expectation made us in a grea[t]
measure to be Pityed : for tho' some were so crue[l]
and barbarous as to take & carry to the door, Tw[o]
of my Children and Murder them, as also a Negr[o]
Woman ; yet they gave me liberty to put on m[y]
Cloths, keeping me bound with a Cord on o[ne]
arm, till I put on my Cloths to the other ; a[nd]
then changing my Cord, they let me dress my se[lf]
and then Pinioned me again. Gave liberty to [my]
dear Wife to dress her self, & our Children. Abo[ut]
Sun an hour high, we were all carryed out of t[he]

hous[e]

House, for a March, and saw many of the Houses of my Neighbours in Flames, perceiving the whole Fort, one house excepted, to be taken. Who can tell, what Sorrows pierced our Souls, when we saw our selves catryed away from Gods Sanctuary, to go into a strange Land, expofed to fo many Trials? The journey being at leaft Three hundred Miles we were to Travel; the Snow up to the Knees, and we never inur'd to fuch hardfhips and fatigues, the place we were to be carryed to, a Popifh Country. Upon my parting from the Town they fired my House & Barn. We were carryed over the River, to the foot of the *Mountain*, about a Mile from my House, where we found, a great number of our Chriftian Neighbours, Men, Women & Children, to the number of an hundred, Nineteen of which were afterward Murdered by the Way, and Two ftarved to Death, near *Cowaſs*, in a time of great fcarcity or Famine, the Salvages underwent there. When we came to the foot of our Mountain, they took away our Shoes, and gave us, in the room of them Indian-Shoes, to prepare us for our Travel. Whilft we were there the Englifh beat out a Company, that remained in the Town, and purfued them to the River, Killing and Wounding many of them; but the body of the Army, being Alarm'd, they repulfed thofe few *Englifh* that purfued them. I am not able to give you an account of the number of the Enemy Slain, but I obferved after this there no great infulting Mirth, as I expected; and many Wounded Perfons, and for feveral days after they buryed of their party, & one of chief

Note.

Note among the *Maqua's*. The Governour of *Canada*, told me, his Army had that Success with the loss but of Eleven men, Three French-men, One of which was the *Lieutenant* of the Army, Five *Maqua's*, and Three *Indians*: but after my Arrival at *Quebeck*, I spake with an English man, who was taken the last War, and Married there, and of their Religion; who told me, they lost above Forty, and that many were Wounded: I replyed the Governour of *Canada* said, they lost but Eleven men: He answered, 'tis true, That there were but Eleven killed out-right at the taking of the Fort, but that many others were Wounded, among whom was the *Ensign* of the *French*; but said he, they had a fight in the Meadow, and that in both Engagements, they lost more than Forty. Some of the Souldiers, both *French* and *Indians* then present told me so (said he) adding, That the French always endeavour, to conceal the number of their Slain.

After this, we went up the Mountain, and saw the smoak of the Fires in the Town, and beheld the awful desolations of our Town: And before we marched any farther, they kill'd a Sucking Child of the English. There were slain by the Enemy of the Inhabitants of our Town to the number of Thirty-eight, besides Nine of the Neighbouring Town. We Travel'd not far the first day; God made the Heathen, so to Pity our Children, that though they had several Wounded Persons, of their own, to carry, upon their Shoulders, for Thirty Miles, before they came to the River, yet they carryed our Children, uncapable of Travelling, upon their Shoulders.

nd in their Arms. When we came to our Lodg-
ng place, the firſt Night, they dugg away the
Snow, and made ſome Wigwams, cut down ſome
of the ſmall branches of *Spruce-trees* to lye down on,
nd gave the Priſoners ſome-what to eat ; but we
had but little Appetite. I was Pinioned, and bound
own that Night, and ſo I was every Night whilſt
was with the Army. Some of the Enemy who
rought drink with them, from the Town, fell to
Drinking, and in their Drunken fit, they kill'd my
Negro man, the only dead Perſon, I either ſaw at
he Town, or in the Way. In the Night an *Eng-
li/h* Man made his eſcape : in the Morning I was
all'd for, and ordered by the General to tell the
Engliſh, That if any more made their eſcape, they
ould burn the reſt of the Priſoners. He that took
me was unwilling to let me ſpeak with any of the
Priſoners, as we March'd ; but on the Morning of
he Second day, he being appointed to guard the
Rear, I was put into the hands of my other Maſter,
Who permitted me to ſpeak to my Wife, when I
vertook her, and to Walk with her to help her in
er Journey. On the Way we diſcourſed of the
appineſs of them who had a right to *an Houſe not
made with Hands, Eternal in the Heavens ;* and *God for
a Father, and Friend ;* as alſo, That it was our rea-
onable Duty, quietly to ſubmit, to the Will of
God, and to ſay, *The Will of the Lord be done.* My
Wife told me her ſtrength of body began to fail, &
hat I muſt expect to part with her ; Saying, She
oped God would preſerve my Life, and the Life of
one, if not of all of our Children, with us ; and
                                                    com-

commended to me, under God, the care of ther
She never spake any discontented Word as to wh
had befal'n us, but with suitable expressions justif
ed God, in what had befal'n us. We soon made a
halt, in which time my chief Surviving Master can
up, upon which I was put upon Marching with th
foremost, and so made to take my last fare-well (
my dear Wife, *the desire of my Eyes*, and companic
in many Mercies and Afflictions. Upon our Sep:
ration from each other, we askt for each othe
Grace sufficient, for what God should call us to
After our being parted from one another, she sper
the few remaining Minutes of her stay, in Readin
the Holy Scriptures; which she was wont Persona
ly every day to delight her Soul in Reading, Pra
ing, Meditating of, and over, by her self, in he
Closet, over and above what she heard out of the
in our Family Worship. I was made to Wade ov
a small River, and so were all the English, the W:
ter above Knee-deep, the Stream very Swift; an
after that, to Travel up a small Mountain, my Streng
was almost spent, before I came to the top of it: N
sooner had I overcome the difficulty of that ascen
but I was permitted to sit down, & be unburthene
of my Pack; I sat pitying those who were behin
and intreated my Master, to let me go down, an
help up my Wife, but he refused, and would not l
me stir from him. I ask'd each of the Prisone
(as they passed by me) after her, and heard that
passing through the abovesaid River, she fell dow
and was plunged over Head and Ears in the Wate
after which she travelled not far, for at the Foot

his Mountain, the cruel and blood thirsty Salvage who took her, flew her with his Hatchet, at one troak; the tidings of which were very awful: and yet such was the hard-heartedness of the Adversary, that my Tears were reckoned to me as a reproach. My loss, and the loss of my Children was great, our hearts were so filled with Sorrow, that nothing but the comfortable hopes of her being taken away in Mercy, to her self, from the evils we were to see, feel and suffer under; (and joyn'd to the Assembly of the *Spirits of just men made perfect,* to rest in Peace, and *joy unspeakable, and full of glory;* and the good pleasure of God thus to exercise us,) could have kept us from sinking under, at that time. That Scripture, *Job* 1. 21. --- *Naked came I out of my Mothers womb, and Naked shall I return thither: the Lord gave, and the Lord hath taken away, blessed be the Name of the Lord;* Was brought to my Mind, and from it, That an *Afflicting God was to be Glorifyed;* with some other places of Scripture, to perswade to a Patient bearing my Afflictions.

We were again call'd upon to March, with a far heavier *Burden on my Spirits,* than on my *Back,* I beg'd of God, to Over-rule in His Providence, that the Corpse of One so dear to me, and of one whose Spirit, He had taken to dwell with Him in Glory, might meet with a Christian burial, and not be left for Meat, to the Fowls of the Air, and Beasts of the Earth; A Mercy that God graciously vouchsafed to grant. For God put it into the hearts of my Neighbours, to come out as far as she lay, to take up her Corpse, recarry it to the Town, and decently to bury

bury it, soon after. In our March they killed another Sucking Infant of one of my Neighbours; and before Night, a Girl of about Eleven years of Age. I was made to Mourn, at the Confideration of my Flocks being fo far a Flock of Slaughter, many being Slain in the Town, and fo many Murdered in fo few Miles from the Town; and from fears what we muft yet expect, from fuch who delightfully imbrued their hands in the blood of fo many of His People. When we came to our lodging Place, an Indian Captain from the *Eaftward* fpake to my Mafter about killing of me, and taking off my Scalp. I lift up my heart to God, to implore His Grace, and Mercy in fuch a time of need; and afterwards I told my Mafter, if he intended to kill me, I defired he would let me know of it, affuring him that my Death after a promife of Quarter would bring the guilt of blood upon him. He told me he would not kill me: We laid down and Slept for God Suftained and kept us. In the Morning we were all called before the chief *Sachems* of the *Macqua's,* and *Indians,* that a more equal diftribution might be made of the Prifoners, among them: at my going from the *Wigwam,* my beft Clothing was taken away from me. As I came nigh the Place appointed, fome of the Captives met me, and told me, they thought the Enemies were going to burn fome of us, for they had peeled off the bark from feveral Trees, and acted very ftrangely. To whom I replyed, They could act nothing againft us, but as they were permitted of God, and I was perfwaded, He would prevent fuch Severities. When we came to the *Wigwam* appointed,

appointed, several of the Captives were taken from
their former Masters, and put into the hands of o-
thers : but I was sent again to my two Masters, who
brought me from my House.

In our fourth days March the Enemy killed another of my Neighbours, who being nigh the time
of Travail, was wearied with her Journey. When we
came to the great River, the Enemy took *Slayes* to
draw their Wounded, several of our Children, and
their Packs ; and Marched a great pace. I Travelled many hours in Water up to the ankles : near
Night I was very Lame, having before my Travel
wrong'd my anckle-bone and sinews: I thought, so
did others, that I should not be able to hold out
to Travel far. I lift up my Heart to God (my only
refuge) to remove my Lameness, and carry me
through with my Children and Neighbours, if He
judg'd it best ; however I desired God would be with
me in my great Change, if He call'd me by such a
Death to Glorify Him : and that He would take care
of my Children, and Neighbours, and bless them ;
and within a little space of time, I was well of my
Lameness, to the joy of my Children, and Neighbours, that saw so great an alteration in my Travelling.

On the Saturday, the Journey was long and
tedious ; we travelled with such speed, that four
Women were tired, and then Slain by them who
led them Captive.

On the *Sabbath Day* we rested, and I was permitted to Pray and Preach to the Captives. The place
of Scripture spoken from, was. *Lam.* 1. 18. *The Lord*

B

is righteous, for I have rebelled against his commandment: Hear, I pray you, all people, and behold my Sorrow: my virgins and my young men are gone into captivity. The Enemy who said to us, *Sing us one of Zions Songs;* were ready some of them, to upbraid us, because our Singing was not so loud as theirs. When the Maquas and Indians were chief in power, we had this revival in our bondage; to joyn together in the Worship of God, and encourage one another to a Patient *bearing the Indignation of the Lord, till he should plead our cause.* When we arrived to *New France* we were forbidden Praying one with another, or joyning together in the Service of God.

The next day, soon after we Marched, we had an Alarm; on which many of the *English* were bound: I was then near the Front, and my Masters not with me; so I was not bound. This Alarm was occasioned by some *Indians* shooting at *Geese* that flew over them, that put them into a considerable consternation, and fright: but after they came to understand they were not pursued by the *English,* they boasted, That the *English* would not come out after them, as they had boasted before, we began our Journey in the Morning. They kill'd this day Two Women, who were so faint they could not Travel.

The next day in the Morning, before we Travelled, one *Mary Brooks,* a pious Young Woman, came to the *Wigwam* where I was, and told me, She desired to bless God, who had inclined the heart of her Master, to let her come to take her farewell of me. Said she, by my falls on the Ice yesterday

wrong

wrong'd my felf, caufing an Abortion this Night, fo that I am not able to Travel far ; I know they will kill me to day : but (fayes fhe) God has (Praifed be His Name) by His Spirit with His Word, ftrengthened me to my laft encounter with Death : and mentioned to me fome places of *Scripture* fo feafonably fent in for her fupport. And (fays fhe) *I am not afraid of Death,* I can through the Grace of God, chearfully fubmit to the Will of God. Pray for me (faid fhe) at parting, That God would take me to Himfelf. Accordingly fhe was killed that day. I mention it to the end, I may ftir up all in their Young Days, to improve the Death of CHRIST by Faith, to a giving them an holy boldnefs in the day of Death.

The next day we were made to Scatter one from another into fmaller Companies ; and one of my Children carryed away with *Indians,* belonging to the *Eaftern* parts. At Night my Mafter came to me, with my Piftol in his hand, and put it to my breaft, and faid, Now I will kill you, for (faid he) at your Houfe you would have killed me with it if you could. But by the Grace of God, I was not much daunted, and whatever his intention might be ; God prevented my Death.

The next day, I was again permitted to *Pray* with that Company of Captives with me, and we allowed to *Sing a Pfalm* together. After which, I was taken from all the Company of the *Englifh,* excepting two Children of my Neighbours, one of which a Girl of four years of Age, was kill'd by next *Aqqua,* Mafter, the next Morning, the fno them.

We

ing so deep, when we left the River, that he could not carry the Child and his Pack too.

When the Sabbath came, one *Indian* staid with me, and a little Boy Nine years old, whilst the rest went a hunting. And when I was here, I thought with my self, that God had now separated me from the Congregation of His People, who were *now* in His *Sanctuary* where He Commandeth the *Blessing, even Life for ever*: And made to bewail my *Unfruitfulness* under, and *Unthankfulness* for such a Mercy. When my Spirit was almost over-whelmed within me at the consideration of what had passed over me, and what was to be expected; I was ready almost to Sink in my Spirit. But God spake those Words with a greater efficacy then man could speak them, for my strengthning and support: *Psal.* 118. 17. *I shall not dye, but live: and declare the works of the Lord. Psal.* 42. 11. *Why art thou cast down, O my Soul? and why art thou disquieted within me? hope thou in God: for I shall yet praise him, who is the health of my countenance, and my God.* Nehem. 1. 8, 9. *Remember I beseech thee, the word that thou commandedst thy Servant Moses, saying, If ye transgress, I will scatter you abroad among the Nations: But if ye turn unto me, and keep my commandments, and do them; though there were of you cast out unto the uttermost part of the heaven, yet will I gather them from thence, and will bring them unto the place that I have chosen, to set my Name there.* These Three places of Scripture, one after another by the *Grace of God,* strengthened my *Hopes,* that God would so far restrain the Wrath of the Adversary, that the greatest number of us left alive, should be carryed

through

through so tedious a Journey. That tho' my Chil-dren had no Father to take care of them, that Word quieted me to a patient waiting to see the end the Lord would make, *Jer.* 49. 11. *Leave thy fatherless Children, I will preserve them alive, and let thy Widows trust in me.* Accordingly God carryed them Won-derfully through great Difficulties and Dangers. My youngest Daughter, Aged *Seven* years, was carryed all the Journey, & look'd after with a great deal of Tenderness. My youngest Son, Aged *Four* years, was Wonderfully preserved from Death ; for though they that carryed him, or draw'd him on *Sleyes*, were tired with their Journeys, yet their Sal-vage cruel Tempers, were so over-ruled by God, that they did not kill him, but in their pity, he was spared, and others would take care of him ; so that four times on the Journey he was spared, and others would take care of him, till at last he arrived at *Mont-Royal*, where a *French* Gentlewoman pitying the Child, redeemed it out of the hands of the Hea-then. My Son *Samuel,* and my Eldest Daughter were pityed, so as to be drawn on *Sleyes,* when un-able to Travel. And tho' they suffered very much through Scarcity of Food, and tedious Journeys, they were carryed through to *Mont-Royal.* And my Son *Stephen* about *Eleven* years of Age, Wonderfully preserved from Death, in the Famine whereof three *English* Persons dyed, and after Eight Months brought into *Shamblee.*

My Master returned on the Evening of the *Sab-bath,* and told me, *be had killed five Moose.* The next day we removed to the place where he killed them.

We

We tarryed there three days, till we had rofted and dryed the Meat. My Matter made me a pair of *Snow-shoes*, for (faid he) *You cannot poffibly Travel without*; the *Snow* being knee-deep. We parted from thence Leavy laden; I Travelled with a burden on my back, with *Snow-shoes Twenty-five* Miles the firft day of wearing them; and again the next day till afternoon; and then we came to the *French River*. My Matter at this place took away my pack, and draw'd the whole load on the Ice: but my bones feemed to be mifplaced and I unable to Travel with any fpeed. My feet were very fore, and each Night I wrung *blood* out of my *Stockings*, when I pulled them off. My *Shins* alfo were very fore, being cut with *Cruffy Snow*, in the time of my Travelling without *Snow-shoes*. But finding fome dry *Oak-leaves*, by the River banks, I put them to my *Shins*, and in once applying of them, they were healed. And here my Matter was very kind to me, would alwayes give me the beft he had to Eat; and by the goodnefs of God, I never wanted a *Meals Meat*, during my Captivity; tho' fome of my Children and Neighbours, were greatly Wounded, (as I may fay) with the Arrows of *Famine*, and *Pinching want*; having for many dayes nothing but *Roots* to live upon, and not much of them neither. My Matter gave me a piece of a BIBLE; never difturbed me in Reading the *Scriptures*, or in *Praying* to God. Many of my Neighbours alfo, found that Mercy in their Journey, to have *Bibles, Pfalm-books, Catechifms, and Good Books*, put into their hands, with Mercy to ufe them; and yet after their Arrival at
Canada,

Canada, all possible endeavours were used, to deprive them of them. Some of them say, their *Bibles* were demanded by the *French Priests*, and never re-delivered to them, to their great grief and sorrow.

My March on the *French River* was very sore, for fearing a *Thaw*, we Travelled a very great pace; my Feet were so bruised, and my joynts so distorted by my Travelling in *Snow-shoes*, that I thought it unpossible to hold out. One Morning a little before break of day, my Master came & awaken'd me out of my Sleep, saying, *Arise, Pray to God, and Eat your Breakfast, for we must go a great way to day.* After Prayer, I arose from my knees, but my feet were so *Tender, Swoln, Bruised,* and full of *Pain,* that I could scarce stand upon them, without holding on the *Wigwam.* And when the *Indians* said, *You must run to day;* I answered, I could not run: My Master pointing out to his Hatchet, said to me, *Then I must dash out your Brains, and take off your Scalp.* I said I suppose then you will do so, for I am not able to Travel with speed. He sent me away alone, on the Ice. About Sun half an hour high, he overtook me, for I had gone very slowly, not thinking it possible to Travel Five Miles. When he came up he called me to *Run;* I told him I could go no faster; he passed by without saying one Word more: So that sometimes I scarce saw any thing of him for an hour together. I Travel'd from about break of day, till dark, never so much as set down at noon to Eat Warm Victuals; Eating frozen Meat, which I had in my Coat Pocket, as I Travel'd. We went that day *Two* of their dayes Journey, as they came down. I judge we went Forty or Forty five Miles that day. God Wonderfully supported me, and so far renewed my Strength; that in the afternoon I was Stronger to Travel than in the forenoon. My Strength was restored and renewed to admiration. We should never distrust the care and compassion of God, who can give *Strength to them who have no might, and power to them who are ready to faint.*

When we entred on the Lake the Ice, was very rough, and uneven, which was very grievous to my feet, that could scarce endure to be set down on the Smooth Ice, on the River ; I lift up my cry to God in Ejaculatory requests, *That He would take notice of my State, and some way or other relieve me.* I had not Marched above half a Mile, before there fell a *Moist Snow*, about an inch and half deep, that made it very soft for my feet, to pass over the Lake, to the place where my Masters Family was. Wonderful favours in the midst of trying Afflictions ! We went a days Journey from the Lake, to a small Company of *Indians*, who were a hunting ; they were after their manner kind to me, and gave me the best they had, which was *Moose-flesh, Ground-nuts* and *Cramberrys*, but no Bread : For Three Weeks together I eat no Bread. After our stay there, and undergoing difficulties in *Cutting of Wood*, and suffering from *Lousiness*, having *Louzy* old Clothes of Souldiers, put upon me, when they stript me of mine, to Sell to the *French* Souldiers in the Army.

We

We again began a March for *Shamblee*, we ſtay'd at a branch of the Lake, and feaſted Two or Three days on *Geeſe* we killed there.   After another days Travel, we came to a River where the Ice was thaw'd, we made a *Cannoe* of *Elm-bark*, in one day ; and arrived on a Saturday near noon at *Shamblee*, a ſmall Village, where is a Gariſon, & Fort of *French* Souldiers.   This Village is about Fifteen Miles from *Mont-Royal*.   The *French* were very kind to me : A Gentleman of the Place, took me into his Houſe, and to his Table ; and lodged me at Night on a good *Feather-bed*.   The Inhabitants, and Officers were very obliging to me, the little time I ſtay'd with them, and promiſed to Write a Letter to the Governour in Chief, to inform him of my paſſing down the River. Here I ſaw a Girl taken from our *Town*, and a young Man, who informed me, that the greateſt part of the *Captives* were come in, and that *Two* of my Children were at *Mont-Royal* ; that many of the Captives had been in, *Three Weeks* before my arrival : Mercy in the midſt of Judgment !   As we paſſed along the River towards *Sorel*, we went into an Houſe where was an *Engliſh Woman* of our *Town*, who had been left among the *French* in order to her Conveyance to the *Indian* Fort.   The *French* were very kind to her, and to my ſelf, and gave us the beſt Proviſion they had ; and ſhe Embarkqued with us to go down to St. *Francois* Fort.   When we came down to the firſt Inhabited Houſe at *Sorel*, a *French* Woman came to the River-ſide, and deſired us to go into her Houſe, and which we were entred, She compaſſioned our State, and told us, *She had in the laſt War been a Captive among*

mong

mong the Indians, and therefore was not a little sensible
our difficulties. She gave the *Indians* something to ea
in the *Chimny corner,* and spread a cloth on the *Tab*
for us with *Napkins;* Which gave such offence t
the *Indians,* that they hasted away, and would no
call in at the Fort. But where-ever we entred int
Houses, the *French* were very Courteous. When w
came to St. *Francis* River, we found some difficult
by reason of the Ice; and entring into a French
mans House, he gave us a loaf of Bread, and som
Fish to carry away with us; but we passed dow
the River till Night, and there Seven of us Suppe
on the Fish, called *Bull-head* or *Pout,* and did not ea
it up, the Fish was so very large.

The next Morning we met with such a grea
quantity of Ice, that we were forced to leave ou
Cannoe, and Travel on Land. We went to a *Frenc*
Officers house, who took us into a private Room
out of the sight of the *Indians,* and treated us ver
Courteously. That Night we arrived at the Fo
call'd St. *Francois;* Where we found several poo
Children who had been taken from the *Eastwar*
the Summer before, a sight very Affecting, they be
ing in habit very much like *Indians,* and in Manne
very much Symbolizing with them. At this Fo
lived two *Jesuits,* one of which was made Superiou
of the *Jesuits* at *Quebeck.* One of these *Jesuits* me
me at the Fort Gate, and asked me to go into th
Church, and *Give God Thanks for preserving my Lif*
I told him I would do that in some other Plac
When the Bell rang for Evening Prayers, he tha
took me, *Bid me go;* but I refused; The Jes
cam

came to our *Wigwam*, and Prayed a short Prayer ; and invited me to Sup with them ; and justifyed the *Indians* in what they did against us : Rehearsing some things done by *Major Walden*, above Thirty years ago ; and how justly God retaliated them in the last War, and inveighed against us for beginning this War with the *Indians*. And said, *We had before the last Winter, and in the Winter been very Barbarous, and Cruel in burning and killing Indians.* I told them, That the *Indians* in a very Perfidious manner, had committed *Murders* on many of our Inhabitants, after the Signing *Articles of Peace* : and as to what they spake of *Cruelties*, they were undoubtedly *Falsehoods*, for I well knew, the *English* were not approvers of any inhumanity, or barbarity towards Enemies. They said, *An English man had killed one of St Casteen's Relations, which occasioned this War* : for, say they, *The Nations in a general Counsel, had concluded not to engage in the War, on any side, till they themselves were first molested, and then all of them as one, would engage against them that began a War with them ; and that upon the killing of* Casteens *Kindsman, a Post was dispatched to* Canada, *to advertise the* Maqua's, *and* Indians, *that the* English *had begun a War. On which they gathered up their Forces, and that the* French *joyned with them, to come down on the* Eastern *Parts ; and that when they came near* New-England, *several of the* Eastern *Indians, told them of the Peace made with the* English, *and the satisfaction given them from the* English *for that Murders. But the* Macqua's *told them, it was now too late ; for they were sent for, and were now come, and would fall on them, if without their consent they made a Peace*
with

with the English. Said alfo, *That a Letter was fhown them fent from the Governour of* Port-Royal, *which h faid, was taken in an* Englifh *Ship, being a Letter fro the Queen of* England, *to our Governour, Writing bo She approved his defigns; to Enfnare and deceitfully to fei on the* Indians *; fo that being inraged from that Lett and being forced as it were, they began the prefent W* I told them the Letter was a *Lye* forged by the *Frenc*

The next Morning the *Bell Rang* for *Mafs :* M Mafter *bid me go to Church :* I refufed : he threatne me, and went away in a rage. At Noon the *Jefui* fent for me, to dine with them ; for I eat at the Table all the time I was at the Fort. And after Dir ner, they told me, *the* Indians *would not allow of a of their Captives ftaying in their* Wigwams, *whilft th were at Church ; and were refolved by force and violen to bring us all to Church, if we would not go witho* I told them it was highly unreafonable fo to impof upon thofe who were of a contrary Religion ; an to force us to be prefent at fuch Service, as we *Ab hor'd,* was nothing becoming Chriftianity. They r plyed, *They were Salvages, and would not hearken to re fon, but would have their* Wills : Said alfo, *If they w in* New-England *themfelves, they would go into th Churches to fee their Wayes of* Worfhip. I anfwered, th cafe was far different, for there was nothing (them felves being judges) as to matter or manner of *Wo fhip,* but what was according to the Word of God, our Churches ; and therefore it could not be an o fence to any mans Confcience. But among thon there were *Idolatrous Superftitions* in *Worfhip* the said, *Come and see, and offer us Conviction, of what is superstitious in Worship.* To which I answered, *That I was not to do Evil that Good might come on it;* and that forcing in matters of Religion was hateful. They answered, *The Indians were resolved to have it so, & they would not pacify them without my coming; and they would engage they should offer no force or violence to cause any compliance with their Ceremonies.*

The next Mass, my Master bid me go to Church: I objected; he arose and forcibly pulled me out by Head and Shoulders out of the *Wigwam* to the Church, that was nigh the door. So I went in and sat down behind the door, and there saw a great confusion, instead of any *Gospel Order.* For one of the *Jesuits* was at the Altar, saying *Mass* in a Tongue *Unknown* to the Salvages, and the other, between the Altar & the door, saying and singing *Prayers* among the *Indians* at the same time; and many others were at the same time saying over their *Pater Nosters*, and *Ave Mary*, by tale from their *Chapelit*, or *Beads* on a string. At our going out we smiled at their Devotion so managed; which was offensive to them: for they said, *We made a Derision of their Worship.* When I was here, a certain Salvagess dyed; one of the *Jesuits* told me, *She was a very holy Woman, who had not committed One Sin in Twelve years.* After a day or two the *Jesuits* ask'd me, *What I thought of their Way, now I saw it?* I told them, I thought Christ said of it, as *Mark* 7. 7, 8, 9. *Howbeit, in vain do they Worship me, teaching for doctrines the Commandments of men. For laying aside the Commandment of God, ye hold the tradition of men, as the washing of pots, and cups: and many other*

such

such 'ike things ye do. And he *said unto them, Full* w
ye reject the commandment of God, that ye may keep yo
own tradition. They told me, *They were not the Com*
mandments of men, but *Apostolical Traditions,* of equa
authority with the Holy Scriptures, And that afte
my Death, I would bewail my not Praying to th
Virgin *Mary ;* and that I should find the want of h
Interceſſion for me, *with her Son ;* judging me t
Hell for aſſerting, the Scriptures to be a perfect rul
of Faith : and ſaid, I abounded in my own ſenſe, en
rertaining explications contrary to the ſenſe of th
Pope, regularly ſitting with a general Council, ex
plaining Scripture, and making Articles of Faith
I told them, It was my Comfort that Chriſt was t
be my *Judge,* and not they at the *Great Day* : An
as for their cenſuring and judging of me, I wa
not moved with it. One day a certain Salvage
taken Priſoner in *Philips* War, who had lived at M
Buckleys at *Wethersfield,* called *Ruth,* who could ſpea
Engliſh very well ; who had been often at my Houſ
but was now proſelyted to the *Romiſh Faith,* cam
into the *Wigwam,* and with her an *Engliſh* Maid
who was taken the laſt War, who was dreſs'd u
in *Indian* Apparel, could not ſpeak one word
Engliſh, who ſaid ſhe could neither tell her ow
name, or the name of the place from whence ſh
was taken. Theſe two talked in the *Indian* Diale
with my Maſter a long time ; after which my Ma
ſter bad me *Croſs my ſelf ;* I told him I would no
he commanded me ſeveral times, and I as often re
fuſed. *Ruth* ſaid, Mr. *Williams* you know the Scri
ture, and therefore act againſt your own light

or you know the Scripture faith, *Servants obey your Masters*; he is your Master, and you his Servant, told her she was ignorant, and knew not the meaning of the Scripture, telling her, *I was not to disobey the Great God to obey any Master, and that I was ready to suffer for God if called thereto*: On which she talked to my Master, I suppose she interpreted what said. My Master took hold of my hand to force me to *Cross my self*, but I strugled with him, and would not suffer him to guide my hand; upon this he pulled off a *Crucifix* from his own neck, and bad me *Kiss* it; but I refused once and again; he told me *he would dash out my brains with his Hatchet if I refused*. I told him I should sooner chuse death then to Sin against God; then he ran and catcht up his Hatchet, and acted as tho' he would have dashed out my Brains; seeing I was not moved, he threw down his Hatchet, saying, *he would first bite off all my nails if I still refused*; I gave him my hand and told him, I was ready to suffer, he set his teeth in my thumb nails and gave a gripe with his teeth, and then said, *no good Minister, no love God, as bad as the Devil*; and so left off. I have reason to bless God who strengthened me to withstand; by this he was so discouraged as never more to meddle with me about my Religion. I askt leave of the *Jesuits* to Pray with those *English* of our Town that were with me, but they absolutely refused to give us any permission to pray one with another, and did what they could to prevent our having any discourse together.

After a few days the Governour *de Vaudrel*, Governour in Chief, sent down two men with Letters to the *Jesuits*, desiring them to order my being sent up to him to *Mont-Royal*, upon which one of the *Jesuits* went with my two Masters, and took me along with them, as also two more of *Deerfield*, a man and his Daughter about *Seven* years of Age. When we came to the Lake, the Wind was tempestuous & contrary to us, so that they were afraid to go over, they Landed and kindled a fire, & said they would wait a while to see whether the Wind would fall or change. I went a side from the Company among the Trees, and spread our case with the temptations of it before God, and pleaded that He would order the season so, that we might not go back again, but be furthered on our Voyage, that I might have opportunity to see my Children and Neighbours, and converse with them, and know their state. When I returned, the Wind was more boisterous, and then a second time, and the Wind was more fierce; I reflected upon my self for my unquietness, and the want of a resigned will to the Will of God. And a third time went & bewailed before God my anxious cares, and the tumultuous workings of my own heart, begg'd a Will fully resigned to the Will of God, and thought that by the Grace of God I was brought to say *Amen*, to whatever God should determine. Upon my return to the Company, the Wind was yet high; the Jesuit and my Master said, come we will go back again to the Fort, for there is no likelihood of proceeding in our Voyage, for very frequently such a Wind continues three days, sometimes six; after it continued so many hours. I said to them, *the Will of the Lord be done;*

and

and the Cannoe was put again into the River, and we embarqued. No fooner had my Mafter put me into the Cannoe, and put off from the Shoar, but the Wind fell, and coming into the middle of the River, they faid, *We may go over the Lake well enough :* and fo we did. I promifed, if God gave me Opportunity I would ftir up others to Glorify God in a continued perfevering, committing their ftraights of heart to Him ; *He is a Prayer bearing God, and the Stormy Winds obey Him.* After we paffed over the Lake, the *French* where ever we came were very compaffionate to us.

When I came to *Mont-Royal*, which was Eight Weeks after my Captivity ; the Governour *de' Vaudrel* redeemed me out of the hands of the *Indians*, gave me good Clothing, took me to his Table, gave me the ufe of a very good Chamber ; and was in all refpects relating to my outward man, courteous and charitable to admiration. At my firft entring into his Houfe, he fent for my two Children, who were in the City, that I might fee them ; and promifed to do what he could to get all my Children & Neighbours out of the hands of the Salvages. My change of Dyet after the difficulties of my Journey's, caufed an alteration in my Body : I was *Phyfick'd, Blooded,* and very tenderly taken care of in my Sicknefs. The Governour redeemed my Eldeft Daughter out of the hands of the *Indians* ; and fhe was carefully tended in the *Hofpital,* until fhe was well of her Lamenefs ; & by the Governour provided for with refpect, during her ftay in the Country. My youngeft Child was redeemed by a Gentlewoman in the City

C

a the _Indians_ paffed by. After the _Indians_ had been at their Fort & difcourfed with the Priefts, they came back and offered to the Gentlewoman a man for the Child, alledging that the Child could not be profitable to her, but the man would, for he was a _Weaver_, and his fervice would much advance the defign fhe had of making cloth : but God over-ruled fo far that this Temptation to the Woman prevailed not for an exchange ; for had the Child gone to the _Indian_ Fort, in an ordinary way it had abode there ftill, as the reft of the Children carryed thither do. The Governour gave orders to certain Officers to get the reft of my Children out of the hands of the _Indians_, and as many of my Neighbours as they could. After Six Weeks a _Merchant_ of the City obtained my Eldeft Son, that was taken to live with him : he took a great deal of pains to perfwade the Salvages to part with him. An _Indian_ came to the City (Sagamore _George_ of _Pennacook_) from _Cowafs_, and brought word of my Son _Stephen's_ being near _Cowafs_, & fom Money was put into his hand for his Redemption and a promife of full fatisfaction if he brought him but the _Indian_ proved unfaithful, and I never faw my Child till a year after. The Governour ordered a Prieft to go along with me to fee my younger Daughter among the _Maqua's_, and endeavour her ranfom. I went with him ; he was very courteous to me, and from his Parifh which was near the _Maqua-_Fort, he wrote a Letter to the _Jefuit_ to defire him to fend my Child to fee me, and to fpeak with them that took her, to come along with it. But the _Jefuit_ wrote back a Letter, _That I fhould not be permitted_

to speak with, or see my Child, if I came that my labour
wou'd be loft ; and that the Macqua's would affoon part
with their hearts, as my Child. At my return to the
City, I with an heavy heart carryed the *Jefuits* Letter to the Governour, who, when he read it, was very angry, and endeavoured to comfort me, affuring
me, *I fhould fee it, and fpeak with it* ; and he would
to his utmoft endeavour its ranfom : Accordingly
he fent to the *Jefuits* who were in the City, and bid
them improve their intereft for the obtaining the
Child. After fome days, he went with me in his
own Perfon to the Fort. When we came thither,
he difcourfed with the *Jefuits*: after which my Child
was brought into the *Chamber* where I was, I was
told I might fpeak with her, but fhould be permitted
to fpeak to no other *Englifh* Perfon there. My Child
was about Seven years old ; I difcourfed with her
near an hour ; fhe could Read very well, and had not
forgotten her *Catechifm* : and was very defirous to
be redeemed out of the hands of the *Macqua's*, and
bemoaned her State among them, telling me how
they prophaned God's *Sabbath's* : and faid, *She thought
that a few days before they had been mocking the Devil,
and that one of the Jefuits ftood and look'd on them*. I
told her, fhe muft Pray to God for His Grace every
day ; She faid, *She did as fhe was able, and God helpt
her* : but, fays fhe, *They force me to fay fome Prayers in
Latin, but I dont underftand one word of them, I hope it
wont do me any harm*. I told her, fhe muft be careful
fhe did not forget her *Catechifm*, and the *Scriptures,*
fhe had learnt by heart. She told the Captives after I was gone, as fome of them have fince informed

me, almost every thing I spake to her ; and said, *She was much afraid she should forget her Catechism,* having none to instruct her. I saw her once a few days after in the City, but had not many Minutes of time with her, but what time I had, I improved to give her the best advice I could. The Governour laboured much for her redemption, at last he had a promise of it, in case he would procure for them an *Indian* Girl in her stead. Accordingly he sent up the River some hundreds of Leagues for one, but it was refused, when offered by the Governour : he offered them an hundred pieces of Eight for her Redemption, but it was refused. His Lady went over to have beg'd her from them, but all in vain ; its there still, and has forgotten to speak *English.* Oh ! that all who peruse this History would joyn in their fervent requests to God, *with whom all things are possible,* that this poor Child, and so many others of our Children who have been *cast upon God from the Womb,* and are now *Out-cast ready to perish,* might be gathered from their dispersions, and receive *Sanctifying Grace* from God ! When I had discoursed with the Child, and was coming out of the Fort, one of the *Jesuits* went out of the Chamber with me, and some Souldiers, to convey me to the *Cannoe.* I saw some of my poor Neighbours, who stood with longing expectations to see me, and speak with me, and had leave from their Salvage Masters so to do. I was by the *Jesuit* himself thrust along by force, and permitted only to tell them some of their Relations (they askt after) were well in the City, and that with a very audible voice, being not permitted to come near to them. Afmy return to the City I was very Melancholly, for I could not be permitted so much as to *Pray* with the *English*, who dwelt in the same house. And the *English* who came to see me, were most of them put back by the Guard at the door, and not suffered to come & speak with me. Sometimes the Guard was so strict that I could scarce go aside on necessary occasions without a repulse ; and whenever I went out into the City (a favour the Governour himself never refused when I ask it of him) there were spies to watch me, and to observe whether I spake to the *English*. Upon which I told some of the *English*, they must be careful to call to mind & improve former Instructions, and endeavour to stand at a further distance for a while, hoping that after a short time I should have more liberty of conversing with them. But some spies sent out, found on a *Sabbath Day* more then *Three* (the number we by their order published were not to exceed together) of us in Company, who informed the Priest ; the next day one of the Priests told me, I had a greater number of the *English* with me, and that I had spoken something reflecting on their *Religion*. I spake to the Governour that no forcible means might be used with any of the Captives respecting their Religion ; he told me, *He allowed no such thing.* I am perswaded that the Governour if he might act as himself, would not have suffered such things to be done as have been done, and that he never did know of several things acted against the *English*.

At my first coming to *Mont-Royal*, the Governour told me, *I should be sent home assoon as Captain* Battiss

was returned and not before ; and that I was taken in or-
der to his Redemption. The Governour fought by all
means to divert me from my Melancholly Sorrows,
and always show'd a willingneſs for ſeeing my Children. And one day I told him of my deſign of
walking into the City ; he pleaſantly anſwered, *Go*
with all my Heart. His Eldeſt Son went with me as
far as the door & ſaw the Guard ſtop me, he went
in and informed his Father, who came to the door
and askt, *Why they affronted the Gentleman going out ?*
They ſaid, *It was their Order :* But with an angry
countenance he ſaid, *His Orders were that I ſhould not*
be ſtopt. But within a little time I had my orders to
go down to *Quebeck.* Another thing ſhowing that
many things are done without the Governours conſent, tho' his Name be uſed to juſtify them, (*viz.*)
I askt the Prieſt, after I had been at *Mont-Royal* two
days, leave to go and ſee my youngeſt Child ; he
ſaid, *When ever you would ſee it tell me, and I will bring*
it to you ; for, ſays he, *The Governour is not willing you*
ſhould go thither. And yet not many days after when
we were at Dinner, the Governours Lady (ſeeing me
ſad) ſpake to an Officer at Table, who could ſpeak
Latin, to tell me, *That after Dinner I ſhould go along*
with them and ſee my two Children. And accordingly
after Dinner I was carryed to ſee them ; and when
I came to the houſe I found three or four Engliſh
Captives who lived there, and I had leave to diſ-
courſe with them. And not long after the Governours Lady askt me, to go along with her to the
Hoſpital to ſee one of my Neighbours Sick there.

One day one of the *Jesuits* came to the Governour, and told the Company there, *That he never saw such Persons as were taken from* Deerfield. Said he, *The* Macqua's *will not suffer any of their Prisoners to abide in their Wigwams whilst they themselves are at Mass, but carry them with them to the Church, and they cant be prevailed with to fall down on their knees to Pray there, but no sooner are they returned to their Wigwams, but they fall down on their knees to Prayer.* He said, *They could do nothing with the grown Persons there ; and they hindred the Childrens complying.* Where-upon, the *Jesuits* counsel'd the *Macqua's* to Sell all the grown Persons from the Fort ; a stratagem to seduce poor Children. *Oh Lord ! Turn the Counsels of these Ahitophels into foolishness, and make the Counsels of the Heathen of none effect !*

Here I observed, they were wonderfully lifted up with Pride, after the return of Captain *Montinug* from *Northampton* with News of Success : they boasted of their Success against *New-England.* And they sent out an Army as they said of Seven hundred men, if I mistake not, Two hundred of which were *French,* in company of which Army went several *Jesuits ;* and said, *They would lay desolate all the Places on* Connecticut *River.* The Superiour of the Priests told me, *Their General was a very Prudent and Brave Commander of undaunted Courage, and he doubted not but they should have great Success.* This Army went away in such a boasting, triumphant manner, that I had great hopes God would discover and disappoint their designs ; our Prayers were not wanting for the blasting such a Bloody design. The Superiour of the

Priests

Priests said to me, *Dont flatter your selves in hopes of a short Captivity*; for, said he, *There are two young Princes contending for the Kingdom of* Spain; *and a Third, that care was to be taken for his Establishment, on the English Throne.* And boasted what they would do to *Europe*; and that we must expect not only *Europe*, but in *New-England* the Establishment of *Popery*. I said, Glory not, God can make great changes in a little time, and revive His own Interest, and yet Save His poor afflicted People. Said he, *The time for Miracles is past*; and in the time of the last War, the *King of France* was as it were against all the World, and yet did very great things, but now the *Kingdom of Spain* is for him, and the *Duke of Bavaria*, and the *Duke of Savoy*, &c. and spake on a lofty manner of great things to be done by them: and having the World as I may say in subjection to them.

I was sent down to *Quebeck* in Company of Governour *de Ramsey* Governour of *Mont-Royal*, and the Superiour of the *Jesuits*, and ordered to live with one of the Council; from whom I received many favours for Seven Weeks. He told me, It was the Priests doings to send me down before the Governour came down; & that if I went much to see the *English*, or they came much to visit me, I should yet certainly be sent away where I should have no converse with the *English*. After my coming down to *Quebeck*, I was invited to Dine with the *Jesuits*, and to my face they were civil enough. But after a few days a young Gentleman came to my Chamber, and told me, that one of the *Jesuits* (after we had done Dinner) made a few Disticks of Verses, & gave them to his Scholars o Tranſlate into *French* : he ſhew'd them to me. The import of them was, " That the King of *France* " his Grand-Son had ſent out his Huntſmen, & that " they had taken a *Wolf*, who was ſhut up, and now " he hopes the Sheep would be in ſafety. I knew at the reading of them what he aimed at, but held my Peace, as tho' I had been ignorant of the *Jeſuits* intention. Obſerving this reproaching Spirit, I ſaid in my Heart, *If God will bleſs, let men curſe if they pleaſe* : and I look'd to God in CHRIST the Great *Shepherd* to keep his ſcattered Sheep among ſo many *Romiſh Revenous Wolves*, and to remember the reproaches wherewith his Holy Name, Ordinances, and Servants were daily reproached. And upon an obſervation of the time of theſe Verſes being compoſed, I find that near the ſame time the *Biſhop* of *Canada* with *Twenty Eccleſiaſticks* were taken by the *Engliſh*, as they were coming from *France*, and carried into *England* as Priſoners of War.

One *Sabbath* day Morning I obſerved many Signs of approaching Rain, a great moiſture on the Stones of the Hearth & Chimny-jams. I was that day invited to Dine with the *Jeſuits* ; and when I went up to Dinner, it began to Rain a ſmall drifling Rain : The Superiour told me, *They had been Praying for Rain that Morning* : *And lo,* (ſays he) *It begins to Rain.* I told him, I could tell him of many inſtances of Gods hearing our Prayers for Rain. However in the afternoon there was a general *Proceſſion* of all orders, *Prieſts, Jeſuits* and *Fryars*, and the *Citizens* in great Pomp, carrying (as they ſaid) as an holy relique, ſome of the bones of St. *Paul*. The next day I was

invited to the Priests Seminary to Dinner ; *Oh,* said
they, *we went in Procession Yesterday for Rain, and see
what a Plentiful Rain followed.* I answered, we had
been answered when Praying for Rain, when no such
Signs of Rain, and the beginnings of Rain preceeded
as now with them, before they appointed or began
their Procession, *&c.* However, they upbraided
me, *That God did not approve of our Religion, in that He
disregarded our Prayers, and accepted theirs. For (* said
they *) We hear you had dayes of Fasting and Prayer before
the Fleet came to* Quebeck ; *God would not regard your
Prayers, but heard ours, & almost in a miraculous way preserved us when assaulted, and refused to hear your Fast-
day-Prayers for your Preservation, but heard ours for
your Desolation, and our Success.* They boasted also of
their *King,* and his greatness, and spake of him as tho'
there could be no Settlement of the World, but as he
pleased ; reviling us as in a low & languishing case,
having no King, but being under the Government of
a *Queen:* And spake as tho' the *Duke* of *Bavaria* would
in a short time be Emperour. From this day for-
ward God gave them to hear sorrowful Tidings from
Europe: That a War was commenced against the
Duke of *Savoy,* and so their Enemies increased,
Their *Bishop* taken, & *Two Millions* of Wealth with him.
News every year more distressing and impoverishing
of them ; and the Duke of *Bavaria* so far from being
Emperour, that he is dispossess'd of his *Dukedom;* & France
so far from being strengthned by *Spain,* that the Kingdom of *Spain* like to be an occasion of the Weakning
and Impoverishing their own Kingdom ; they themselves so reporting. And their great Army &

against *New-England* turn'd back aſhamed; and they
diſcouraged and diſhearten'd, and every year very
exerciſing fears & cares, as to the *Salvages* who live
up the River.   Before the return of that Army, they
told me, We were led up & down and Sold by the
Heathen, as Sheep for the Slaughter, and they could
not deviſe what they ſhould do with us, we ſhould be
ſo many Priſoners, when the Army returned.   The
Jeſuit told me, It was a great Mercy that ſo many of
our Children were brought to them, and that now
eſpecially ſince they were not like ſpeedily to be returned, there was hope of their being brought over
to the *Romiſh Faith.*   They would take the *Engliſh*
Children born among them, and againſt the conſent
of their Parents *Baptize* them.   One *Jeſuit* came to
me and askt, whether all the *Engliſh* at *Loret,* (a place
not far from *Quebeck* where the Salvages lived) were
Baptized ? I told him they were.   He ſaid if they be
not, let me know of it, that I may Baptize them, for
fear they ſhould dye and be damn'd, if they dyed
without Baptiſm.   Says he, *When the Salvages went*
againſt you, I charg'd them to Baptiſe all Children before
they killed them : ſuch was my deſire of your Eternal Sal-
vation tho you were our Enemies.   There was a Gentleman called Monſier *de Beauville,* a Captain, the Brother of the *Lord Intendant,* who was a good friend to
me, and very courteous to all the Captives; he lent
me an *Engliſh* Bible, and when he went to *France* gave
it me.

All means were uſed to ſeduce poor Souls.

I was invited one day to Dine with one of Chief
Note. as I was going, met with the Superior of the

Jefuits coming out of the House, and he came i
after dinner; and prefently it was propounded t
me, if I would ftay among them and be of their Re
ligion, I fhould have a great and honourable Penf
on from the *King* every year.   The Superior of th
Jefuits turned to me, and faid, 'Sir, you have m
'nifefted much grief and forrow for your feparatio
'from fo many of your Neighbours and Children
'if you will now comply with this offer and propo
'fal, you may have all your Children with you
'and here will be enough for an honourable main
'tainance for you and them.   I anfwered, *Sir*, If
thought your Religion to be true, I would imbrac
it freely without any fuch offer, but fo long as
believe it to be what it is, the offer of the whol
World is of no more value to me than a *Blackberry*
and manifefted fuch an abhorrence of this propofal
that I fpeedily went to take my leave and be gone
Oh! *Sir* (faid he) *fet down, why in fuch a hurry, yo
are alone in your Chamber, divert your felf a little longer*
and fell to other difcourfe, and within half an hou
fays again: Sir, I have one thing earneftly to re
queft of you, I pray pleafure me! I faid, let you
Lordfhip fpeak; (faid he,) I pray come down t
the Palace to morrow morning, and honour me
with your Company in my *Coach* to the grea
Church, it being then a *Saints* day.   I anfwere
ask me any thing wherein I can ferve you with
good Confcience, and I am ready to gratifie you
but I muft yet ask your excufe here; and immedi
ately went away from him.   Returning unto
Chamber, I gave God thanks for his upholdin

me, and also made an enquiry with my self, whether I had by any action given encouragement for
such a temptation. Not many days after, and a
few days before Governour *de' Vaudrel* coming down,
I was sent away Fifteen Miles down the River,
that I might not have opportunity of converse with
the *English.* I was courteously treated by the *French,*
and the Priest of that Parish ; they told me he was
one of the most Learned men in the Country ; he
was a very ingenious man, zealous in their way,
but yet very familiar. I had many disputes with the
Priests who came thither, & when I used their own
Authors to confute some of their Positions ; my
Books borrowed of them were taken away from me,
for they said, *I made an ill use of them.* They having
many of them boasted of their Unity in Doctrine
and Profession, were loth I should show them from
their own best approved Authors, as many different
Opinions, as they could charge against us. Here
again, a Gentleman in the presence of the Old Bishop and a Priest, offered me his House, and whole
Living, with assurance of *Honour, Wealth* and *Em-
ployment,* if I would imbrace their ways. I told them,
I had an indignation of Soul against such offers on
such terms, as parting with what was more valuable
than all the World ; alleadging, *What is a man profited
if he gain the whole World, & lose his own Soul ? or what
shall a man give in exchange for his Soul?* I was sometimes told, I might have all my Children if I would
comply, and must never expect to have them on a-
ny other terms ; I told them, my Children were dea-
rer to me than all the world, but I would not deny
Christ

Christ and his *Truths* for the having of them with
me ; *I would still put my trust in God who could perform*
all things for me.

I am perswaded that the Priest of that Parish where
I kept, abhorred their sending down the Heathen to
commit Outrages against the *English*, saying, *it was*
more like committing Murders, than managing a War. In
my Confinement in this Parish, I had my undistur-
bed opportunities to be humbly imploring Grace
for our selves, for Soul and Body, for His protecting
presence with *New-England*, and His disappointing
the bloody designs of Enemies ; that God would be a
little Sanctuary to us in a Land of Captivity, and
that our Friends in *New-England*, might have Grace
to make a more thankful and fruitful improvement
of means of Grace than we had done ; who by our
neglects find our selves out of Gods Sanctuary.

On the Twenty-first of *October*, 1704. I received
some Letters from *New-England*, with an account
that many of our Neighbours escaped out of the desolations in the Fort, and that my *Dear Wife* was re-
carried and decently *Buried.* And that my Eldest Son
who was absent in our desolation, was sent to *Colledge*
and provided for ; which occasioned Thanksgiving
to God in the midst of Afflictions, and caused *Prayer*
even in *Canada*, to be going daily up to Heaven for a
Blessing upon *Benefactors*, showing such kindness to
the desolate and afflicted. The consideration of
such crafty designs to ensnare young ones, and to
turn them from the *Simplicity of the Gospel*, to *Romish*
Superstition, was very exercising ; sometimes they
would

would tell me my Children, sometimes my Neighbours were turned to be of their Religion. Some made it their work to allure poor Souls by flatteries and great promises, some threatned, some offered abusive carriages to such as refused to go to Church and be present at Mass ; for some they industriously contrived to get them Married among them. A Priest drew up a *Compendium* of the *Romish Catholick Faith*, and pretended to prove it by the Scriptures, telling the *English, that all they required was contained in the Scriptures, which they acknowledged to be the Rule of Faith and Manners* ; but it was by Scriptures horribly perverted and abused. I could never come to the sight of it, (tho' I often earnestly entreated a Copy of it) until I was a Shipboard for our Voyage for *New-England* ; but hearing of it, I endeavoured to possess the *English* with their danger of being cheated with such a pretence. I understood they would tell the *English* that I was turn'd, that they might gain them to change their Religion ; these their endeavours to seduce to *Popery* were very exercising to me. And in my Solitariness I drew up these following Sorrowful, Mournful, Considerations, tho' unus'd to, & unskilful in *Poetry*, yet in a plain stile for the use of some of the Captives, who would sometimes make their secret Visits to me, which at the desire of some of them, are here made publick.

Some Contemplations of the Poor, and desolate State of the Church at Deerfield.

THe Sorrows of my heart, enlarged are,
   Whilst I, my present State, with past compare,

I

I frequently, unto Gods House did go,
With Christian Friends, his Praises forth to show,
But now, I Solitary sit, both sigh and cry,
Whilst my Flocks Misery, think on do I.
    Many, both Old & Young, were slain out-right
Some in a bitter Season, take their flight.
Some burnt to Death, and others stifled were,
The Enemy, no Sex, or Age would spare.
The tender Children, with their Parents sad,
Are carry'd forth as Captives, some unclad.
Some Murdered in the Way, unburyed left,
And some thro' Famine, were of Life bereft.
After a tedious Journey, some are Sold,
Some kept in *Heathen* hands, all from Christ fold:
By *Popish rage*, and *Heath'nish* crueltie,
Are banished.   Yea some compell'd to be;
Present at *Mass*. Young Children parted are,
From Parents, and such as instructors were.
Crafty designs are us'd by *Papists* all,
In ignorance of Truth, them to inthrall.
Some threatned are, unless they will comply,
In heathens hands, again be made to lye.
To some, large Promises are made, if they,
Will Truths renounce, and chuse their *Popish* way
    Oh Lord! mine eyes on Thee, shall waiting be,
Till Thou again turn our Captivitie.
Their *Romish* Plots, Thou canst confound ; and Say
This little Flock, this Mercy I do crave.
Save us, from all our Sins, and yet again,
Deliver us from them who Truth disdain.
    Lord! for thy Mercy sake, thy Cov'nant mind
And in thy House, again rest let us find.

So we thy Praifes forth will fhew, and fpeak,
Of all thy Wondrous Works, yea we will feek,
Th'advancement of thy great and glorious Name,
Thy Rich, and Sovereign Grace, we will proclaim.

THe Hearts of fome were ready to be difcouraged & fink, faying, *They were out of fight, and
fo out of mind.* I endeavoured to perfwade them, we
were not forgotten, that undoubtedly many Prayers were continually going up to Heaven for us.
Not long after came Capt. *Livingfton*, and Mr. *Sheldon*, with Letters from His *Excellency* our GOVER-
NOUR, to the Governour of *Canada*, about the
Exchange of Prifoners ; which gave a revival to
many, and raifed expectations of a return. Thefe
vifits from *New-England* to *Canada* fo often, greatly
ftrengthened many who were ready to faint ; and
gave fome check to the defigns of the *Papifts* to gain
Profelytes. But Gods time of deliverance was not
yet come, as to fome particular Perfons, their Temptations & Tryals were increafed ; and fome abufed
becaufe they refufed a compliance with their Superftitions. A young Woman of our Town met with
a new Trial. For on a day, a *French* man came into
the room where fhe was, and fhewed her his *Beads*, &
boafted of them, putting them near to her ; She
knock'd them out of his hands on the floor ; for
which fhe was beaten, and threatned with Death,
and for fome dayes imprifoned. I pleaded with God,
His over-ruling this firft Effay for the deliverance
of fome, as a pledge of the reft being delivered in
due time. I improved Capt. *de Beauville* who had
D   alwayes

alwayes been very friendly, to interceed with the Governour for the return of my Eldeft Daughter; and for his purchafing my Son *Stephen*, from the *Indians* at St. *Francis* Fort; and for liberty to go up and fee my Children and Neighbours at *Mont-Royal*. Divine Providence appeared in a moderating my Affliction, in that *Five* Englifh Perfons of our Town were permitted to return with Capt. *Livingfton*, among whom went my Eldeft Daughter. And my Son *Stephen* was redeemed and fent to live with me: he was almoft quite Naked, and very Poor; he had fuffered much among the *Indians*. One of the *Jefuits* took upon him, to come to the *Wigwam* and Whip him, on fome complaint that the *Squaws* had made, that he did not Work enough for them. As to my Petition for going up to *Mont-Royal* to fee my Children, and Neighbours, it was denyed; as my former defire of coming up to the City before Capt. *Livingftons* coming was. God granted me favour as to Two of my Petitions, but yet brought me by His Grace to be willing, that He fhould glorify Himfelf in difpofing of me and mine as He pleafed, and knew to be moft for His glory: And almoft always before any remarkable favour, I was brought to lye down at the foot of God, and made to be willing that God fhould govern the World, fo as might be moft for His own Honour, and brought to refign all to His holy Sovereignty. A frame of Spirit when wrought in me by the Grace of God, giving the greateft content and fatisfaction, and very often a fore-runner of the Mercy ask'd of God, or a plain demonftration, that the not obtaining of requeft was beft for me. I had no fmall refreshing, in having one of my Children with me for four Months. And the *English* were many of them firengthned with hopes, that the treaty betwixt the Governments would iffue in opening a door of e-fcape for all.

In *August*, Mr. *Dudley* and Capt. *Vetch* arrived, & great incouragements were given as to an Exchange of all in the Spring of the year : and fome few again were fent home ; among whom I obtained leave to fend my Son *Stephen*. Upon Mr. *Dudley's* and Capt. *Vetch's* Petitioning, I was again permitted to go up to *Quebeck* ; but difputing with a *Mendicant Fryar*, who faid, *He was an English-man fent from* France, *to endeavour the Converfion of the* English *at* Quebeck ; Who arrived at *Canada* whilft our Gentlemen were there : I was by the Priefts means ordered again to return to *Chateauviche*, and no other reafon given, but becaufe I difcourfed with that Prieft, and their fear I fhould prevent his fuccefs amongft the Cap-tives. But God fhew'd His diflike of fuch a Perfe-cuting Spirit : for the very next day which was *Sep-tember* 20. *O. S. October* 1ft *N. S.* the *Seminary*, a very famous building, was moft of it burnt down ; occa-fioned by a Joyners letting a Coal of fire drop down among the Shavings. The *Chappel* in the *Priefts* Gar-den, and the *Great Crofs* were burnt down ; the *Li-brary* of the Priefts burnt up : This *Seminary* and a-nother *Library* had been burnt but about Three years before. The day after my being fent away by the Priefts means from *Quebeck* at firft, there was a Thun-der Storm, and the Lightning ftruck the *Seminary* in the very place where the fire now began.

A little before Mr. *Dudley*'s arrival, came a Souldier into my Land-lords house *Bare-foot*, and *Bare-leg'd*, going on a Pilgrimage to *Saint Anne*. For said he, *My Captain who dyed some years ago appeared to me, and told me, he was in Purgatory; and told me I must go a Pilgrimage to Saint Anne, doing Penance, and get a Mass said for him, and then he should be delivered.* And many believed him, and were much affected with it; came and told me of it, to gain my Credit of their devised *Purgatory*: the Souldier told me, *The Priests had counselled him to undertake this Pilgrimage.* And I am apt to think, ordered his calling in at my Land-lords, that I might see and speak with him. I laught at the conceit, that a Souldier must be pitcht upon to be sent on this errand; but they were much displeased, and lamented my obstinacy, in that I would not be reclaimed from a denyal of *Purgatory*, by such a *Miraculous Providence*.

As I was able, I spread the case before God, beseeching of him to disappoint them of their expectations, to Proselyte any of the Captives by this Stratagem; and by the goodness of God it was not very Serviceable: for the Souldiers Conversation was such, that several among the *French* themselves judged it to be a *Forgery*. And tho' the Captain spoken of was the Governours Lady's Brother, I never more heard any concernment or care to get him out of *Purgatory*.

One of the Parish where I lived, told me, That on the *Twenty-second of July*, 1705. He narrat-

beck, at the *Mendicant Fryars Church,* on one of their *Feaſt Days,* in honour of a great *Saint* of *their Order,* and that at Five a Clock Maſs in the Morning, near Two hundred Perſons preſent, A great *Grey Catt* brake or puſh'd aſide ſome Glaſs, and entred into the Church, and paſs'd along it near the Altar, and put out Five or Six Candles, that were burning ; and that no one could tell which way the *Catt* went out : and he thought it was the Devil.

When I was in the City in *September,* I ſaw two *Engliſh* Maids who had lived with the *Indians* a long time. They told me, that an *Indian* had dyed at the place where they were ; and that when ſundry of his Relations were together in order to his burial, the *Dead aroſe,* and informed them, *That at his Death he went to Hell, and there he ſaw all the Indians that had been Dead ſince their embracing the Popiſh Religion ; and warned them to leave it off, or they would be Damned too,* and lay down Dead again. They ſaid, the *Indians* were frightned, & very Melancholly ; but the *Jeſuit* to whom they told this, told them, *It was only a deluſi- on of the Devil to draw them away from the true Religion ;* Adding, *That he knew for certain that all thoſe* Indians *who had been Dead ſpoken of by the* Indian, *were in Heaven, only one Squaw was gone to Hell who dyed with- out Baptiſm.* Theſe Maids ſaid alſo, That many of the *Indians* much Lamented their making a War a- gainſt the *Engliſh,* at the inſtigation of the *French.*

The Prieſts, after Mr. *Dudley's* going from *Canada,* was ready to think their time was ſhort, for gaining *Engliſh* Proſelytes, and doubled their diligence and wiles,

wiles, to gain over Persons to their Perswasion. I improved all opportunities I could, to Write to the *English*, that in that Way I might be Serviceable to them. But many or most of my Letters treating about Religion were intercepted, and burnt. I had a Letter sent down to me by order of the Governour, that I had a liberty of Writing to my Children and Friends, which should be continued; provided I Wrote about indifferent things, and said nothing in them about the points in controversy between them and us: And if I were so hardy as to Write Letters otherwise, they should endeavour to prevent their being delivered. Accordingly, I found many of them were burnt. But sometimes notice would be given to the *English*, that there were Letters written, but that they were burnt; so that their Writing was somewhat useful tho' never perused by the *English*, because they judged those Letters condemned *Popery*. Many of our Letters Written from *New-England*, were never delivered, because of some expressions about Religion in them. And as I said before, after Mr. *Dudley*'s departure from *Quebeck* endeavours were very vigorous to seduce. Some were flattered with large Promises, others were threatned, and beaten, because they would not turn. And when two *English* Women, who had alwayes opposed their Religion were sick in the *Hospital*: they kept with them Night and Day, till they dyed; & their friends kept from coming to visit them: after their death they gave out, that they dyed in the *Romish Faith*, and were received into their *Communion*. Before their Death Masses were said for them; & the buried in the *Church-yard* with all their Ceremonies. And after this, Letters sent into all parts to inform the *English*, that these two Women turn'd to their Religion, before their Death , and that it concern-ed them to follow their Example, for they could not be more obstinate than those Women were in their Health, against the *Romish* Faith, and yet on a D ath bed imbraced it. They told the *English* who lived near, *That our Religion was a dangerous Religion to dye in.* But I shall hereafter relate the just grounds we have to think these things were falsehoods.

I was informed, there was an *English* Girl bid to take and wear the *Cross*, and *Cross her self*: She re-fused ; they threatned her, and showed her the *Cross*. At length, She had her choice, either to *Cross herself*, and take the *Cross*, or be *Whipt*, she chose to be *Whipt* ; and they took up her Clothes, and made as tho' they would correct her ; but seeing her chusing indeed to suffer rather than comply, they desisted and tyed the *Cross* about her Neck. Some were taken & shut up among their Religious, and all sorts of means used to gain them.

I received a Letter from one of my Neighbours, wherein he thus bewails. ' I obtained leave of my ' Master, to go to the *Maequa*-Fort to see my Chil-' dren, that I had not seen for a long time : I car-' ried a Letter from my Master, to shew, that I had ' leave to come. When I came to the Fort, I heard ' one of my Children was in the Woods. I went to ' see a Boy I had there, who lived with one of the ' *Jesuits* ; I had just askt him of his Welfare ; he said ' his Master would come presently ; he durst not stay

' to speak with me now, being in such awe of his
' Master. On which I withdrew, and when his Mas-
' ter came in, I went and askt leave of him to speak
' with my Child, and shewed him my Letter. But he
' absolutely refused to let me see or speak with him;
' and said, I had brought no Letter from the Gover-
' nour, and would not permit me to stay in the Fort,
' tho' I had Travelled on foot near Fifty Miles for
' no other errand than to see and speak with my
' Children.

The same Person with another *English* man last
Spring, obtained leave of the Governour General,
to go to the same Fort on the same errand, & carried
Letters from the Governour to the *Jesuits*, that he
might be permitted to speak with his Children. The
Letter was deliver'd to the *Jesuits*; who told him,
his Son was not at home, but gone a Hunting.
Whenas he was hid from them, as he heard afterward, so the poor man lost his labour a second
time. These men say, that when they returned to
Mont-Royal, one *Laland*, who was appointed as a spy,
always to observe the motions of the *English*, told
them, that one of the *Jesuits* had come in before
them, and had told the Governour that the Lad was
gone out a Hunting. And that the *English* man who
accompanyed this poor man, went out into the
Woods in hopes of finding the Lad; and saw him,
but the Lad run away, and that he followed him &
call'd after him, but he would not stop; but holding
out a Gun threatned to shoot him down, if he followed him, and so he was discouraged, and turn'd back.
And says *Laland, You will never leave going to see your*
Children

Children & Neighbours, till some of you are kill'd. But the men told him, it was an absolute lye, let who would report it; for they had neither seen the Lad, nor did they go into the Woods to search after him. They judge this was told to the Governour, to prevent a-ny English for the future going to see their Children and Neighbours. Some of ours say, they have been little better than absolutely promised, to have their Children who are among the Salvages, in case they themselves would imbrace Popery. And that the Priests had said, *They had rather the Children should be among the Indians, as they did, than be brought out by the French, and so be in a readiness to return for New-England.*

A *Maid* of our Town was put into a Religious house among the *Nuns*, for more than two years, and all sort of means, by flatteries, threatnings, and abusive carriages used to bring her to turn. They offered her Money, which when refused, especially the latter part of the time, they threatned her very much; sent for her before them, commanded her *to Cross her self.* She refused, they hit her a box on the Ear; bid her again, still she refused. They or-dered a rod with Six branches full of knots to be brought; and when she refused, they struke her on the hands, with their renewing their Commands; and she stood to her refusals, till her hands were fill'd with Whales, with the blows. But one said, Beat her no more, we will give her to the *Indians,* if she wont turn. They pinch'd her Arms till they were black & blue; and made her go into their Church, and because she would not *Cross her self,* struke her

several

several blows with their hands on her face.   A *Squaw*
was brought in and said, *She was sent to fetch her to
the Indians* : but she refused ; the *Squaw* went away,
and said, *She would bring her Husband with her to Morrow, and she should be carried away by force.*   She told
me, She remembred what I told her one day, after
the *Nuns* had threatned to give her away to the *Indians* ; that they only said so to affright her, that
they never would give her away.   The *Nuns* told
her, *She should not be permitted any more to speak to the
English ; and that they would afflict her without giving
her any rest, if she refused* : but God preserved her
from falling.   This poor Girl had many Prayers going up to Heaven for her daily, and by name, because her Trials were more known to some of the
English, than the Trials of others, who lived more remote from them.

Here might be an *History* by it self, of the Trials
and Sufferings of many of our Children, and Young
ones, who have been abused, and after Separation
from grown Persons, made to do as they would have
them.

I shall here give an account of what was done to
one of my Children, a Boy between Fifteen and
Sixteen years of Age, Two hundred Miles distant
from me, which occasioned grief and sorrow, that
I want Words to utter ; and yet kept under such
awe, that he never durst Write any thing to me, in
fear of being discovered in Writing about Religion.
They threatned to put him to the *Indians* again, if
he would not turn ; telling him, *He was never bought
out of their hands, but only sojourned with them, but if*

would turn, *he should never be put into their hands any more.* The Priests would spend whole dayes in urging of him. He was sent to School to learn to *Read* and *Write French*; the School-master sometimes flattered him with Promises, if he would *Cross* himself, then threatned him if he would not. But when he saw flattering Promises of rewards, and threatnings were ineffectual, he struke him with a stick he had in his hand; and when he saw that would not do, he made him get down on his knees about an hour, and then came and bid him make the sign of the *Cross*, and that without any delay; he still refused. Then he gave him a couple of Strokes, with a Whip he had in his hand; which Whip had three Branches and about twelve great knots ty'd in it. And again bid him make the *Sign of the Cross*; and if it was any *Sin,* he would bear it himself: and said also, *You are afraid you shall be changed if you do it :* but (said he) *You will be the same, your Fingers wont be changed.* And after he had made him shed many Tears, under his abuses and threatnings, he told him, *He would have it done :* And so thro' Cowardise and Fear of the Whip, he made the Sign. And did so for several dayes together with much ado, he was brought to *Cross* himself. And then the Master told him, *He would have it done without his Particular bidding him.* And when he came to say his Lesson and Cross'd not himself, the Master said, *Have you forgot what I bid you do.* No Sir, said he, Then the School-master said, *Down on your Knees ;* and so kept him for an hour and half, till School was done : and so did for about a Week. When he saw this would not do, he

took

took the Whip, *What wont you do it* (said he) *I will make you*: and so again, frighted him to a compliance. After this, Commanded him to go to the Church: when he refused, he told him, *he would make him.* And one Morning sent four of the biggest Boys of the School, to draw him by force to *Mass.* These, with other severities and witty stratagems were used; and I utterly ignorant of any attempt made upon him, to bring him to change his Religon. His fear was such, that he never durst Write any of these things, least his Letters should fall into their hands, and he should again be deliver'd to the *Indians.* Hearing of an opportunity of Writing to him by one of the Parish where I was, going up to *Mont-Royal.* I Wrote a Letter to him, and had by him a Letter from my Son; which I shall here insert.

' *Honoured Father,*

'I Have received your Letter bearing date *January 11th.* 1705, 6. for which I give you many 'thanks, with my Duty, and my Brothers. I am 'sorry you have not received all the Letters I have 'Writ to you; as I have not received all yours 'According to your good Counsel, I do almost eve'ry day read something of the *Bible,* and so strength'then my faith. As to the Captives newly brought, '*Lancaster* is the Place of two of them, and *Marlbo*'rough that of the third; the Governour of *Mont*'*Royal* has them all three. There is other News 'that will seem more strange to you. That two '*English* Women, who in their Life time were dread'fully set against the *Catholick Religion,* did on their

'death-

death-bed imbrace it. The one *Abigail Turbet*, the other of them *Esther Jones*, both of them known to you. *Abigail Turbet* sent for Mr. *Meriel* the Sabbath before she dyed. Said (many a time upon several following days) *That she committed her Soul into his hands, & was ready to do whatever he pleased.* She desired him to go to the Chappel St. *Anne*, & there to say a *Holy Mass* for her, that she might have her Sins Pardoned, and the Will of the Lord accomplished upon her. Her Cousin Mrs. *Badston*, now *Stilson*, askt her, *Whether she should be willing to do as she said;* She answered, yes. And upon the *Tuesday* she was taken into the *Catholick Church*, in the presence of *John Laland*, and Madam *Grizalem*, an *English* Women, and Mrs. *Stilson*, also with many *French* People besides. She was anointed with *Oyl* on the same day; according to her Will then, upon the *Wednesday* an Image of *Christ Crucifyed*, was brought to her, she caused it to be set up over against her at the Curtains of her bed, and look d continually upon the same; and also a little *Crucifix* brought unto her, she took it, and kissed it, and laid it upon her Stomack. She did also make the sign of the Cross upon her self, when she took any Meat or Drink. She promised to God that if she should recover, she would go to the *Mass* every day: She having on her hand a *Crucifix*, saying, *Oh my Lord that I should have known thee so late!* She did also make a Prayer to the *Virgin Mary*, the two last days of the Week. She could utter no Word, but by kissing the *Crucifix* endeavouring the Crossing her self, she gave an evidence of her faith; she dyed Satur-

'*day*

' day the 24th. of *November*, at three a Clock in the
' afternoon. The next day, the *Priest* did commend
' that Womans Soul to the Prayers of the Congre-
' gation in the *Mass*, in the afternoon she was ho-
' nourably buried in the Church-yard next to the
' Church, close to the body of the Justice *Pese* Wife,
' all the People being present at her Funeral. The
' same day in the Evening, Mr. *Meriel* with an *Eng-*
' *lish* Woman, went to *Esther Jones*; she did at first
' disdain, but a little after she confess'd, there were
' Seven Sacraments, *Chrifts Body present*, the *Sacrament*
' of the *Mass*, the *Inequality of Power among the Pastors*
' of the Church ; and being returned to wait by her
' all Night long, he read & expounded to her some
' part of the *Catholick Confession of Faith* to her satis-
' faction. About Midnight he ask'd her, *Whether she*
' *might not confess her Sins* ; I doubt not but I may,
' said she : And two hours after, she made unto him
' a fervent confession of all the Sins of her whole
' Life. When he said, *How was to offer Christ to his*
' *Father for her* ; She liked it very well. The Supe-
' riour of the *Nuns* being come in to see her, she
' now desired that she might receive Chrifts Body
' before she dyed. She did also show Mrs. *Stilson*, a
' great mind to receive the Sacrament of *Extream*
' *Unction*, and said, *That if ever she should recover and*
' *get home, she would have reproached the Ministers, for*
' *their neglecting that Sacrament so plainly commanded by*
' St. *James*. In the afternoon, after she had beg'd
' pardon for her wavering, and the Catholick Con-
' fession of Faith was read aloud to her, in the hear-
' ing of Mr. *Crofton*, Mrs. *Stilson*, and another *English*
' Woman,

Woman, and she owned the same; about Seven a Clock the same day she said to Mr. *Dubison, Shall not they give me the holy Communion !* But her Tongue was then so thick that she could hardly swallow any thing. She was then anointed with *Holy Oyl* : but before, she said to Mr. *Meriel, Why have you not yet, Sir, forgiven my sins ?* In the Night following, that Priest, and Mr. *Dubison* were continually by her ; and sometimes Praying to God in her name, and Praying to the *Virgin Mary*, and other *Saints.* She said also, *I believe all : I am very glad Christ was offred to his Father for me.* Six or Seven Hours before she dyed, a *Crucifix* was show'd to her by Mr. *Dubison*, she took it and laid it upon her heart, and kiss'd it ; and then the *Nuns* hanging it with a pair of *Beads* upon her Neck. A little before she dyed Mr. *Dubison* askt her to *Pray for him in Heaven* ; she promised him : so she gave up the Ghost, at *Ten* of the Clock the 27*th.* of *November*, whilst the high *Mass* was saying ; she was soon commended to the Prayers. On the fourth day of the Week following was buried ; after the *Mass* had been said for her : she was laid by *Abigail Turbet.*   *Jan.* 23*d.* 1705, 6.

I Have here transcribed the Letter in the very words of it without the least alteration : the same for substance was sent to several other Captives. When I had this Letter, I presently knew it to be of Mr. *Meriels* composing ; but the Messenger who brought the Letter brought word that my son had imbraced their Religion. Afterwards when

some

some blamed him for letting me know of it, because (they said) they feared my Sorrow would shorten my days. He told me, he thought with himself that if he was in my case, he should be willing to know the worst, and therefore told me as he would have desired to have known if in my place. I thank'd him, acknowledging it a favour to let me know of it : But the News was ready to Over-whelm me with Grief and Sorrow. *I made my complaint to G O D, and Mourned before Him ; Sorrow and Anguish took hold upon me.* I ask'd of God to direct me what to do, and how to Write, and find out an opportunity of conveying a Letter to him ; and committed this difficulty to his Providence. I now found a greater opposition to a Patient, Quiet, Humble, Resignation to the Will of God than I should otherwise have known, if not so tryed. Here I thought of my Afflictions and Tryals ; my Wife and Two Children kill'd, and many of my Neighbours ; and my self so many of my Children and Friends in a Popish Captivity, separated from our Children, not capable to come to them to instruct them in the Way they ought to go ; and cunning crafty Enemies, using all their subtilty to insinuate into Young ones, such Principles as would be pernicious. I thought with my self how happy many others were, in that they had their Children with them, under all advantages to bring them up in the *Nurture and Admonition of the Lord.* Whilest we were separated, one from another, and our Children in great Peril of imbracing damnable doctrines. *Oh ! that all Parents who Read this History would Bless God for the advantage*

they have of *Educating their Children, and faithfully improve it* !   I Mourned when I thought with my felf
that I had one Child with the *Macqua's*, a fecond
turn'd to *Popery*, and a little Child of Six years of
Age, in danger from a Child to be inftructed in *Popery*; and knew full well that all endeavours would
be ufed to prevent my feeing or fpeaking with them.
But in the midft of all thefe God gave me a fecret
hope, that He would magnify His Power and free
Grace, and difappoint all their crafty defigns, *When
I look'd on the right hand and on the left, all refuge failed,
and none fhewed any care for my Soul.* But God brought
that Word to uphold me ; *Who is able to do exceeding
abundantly above what we can ask or think.* As alfo
that, *Is any thing too hard for God ?* I Pray'd to God
to direct me ; and Wrote very fhort the firft time,
and in general terms, fearing leaft if I fhould Write
about things in controverfy, my Letters would not
come to him. I therefore addrefs'd him with the
following Letter.

Son Samuel,

YOurs of *January* 23*d.* I received, and with it had
    the Tidings that you had made an abjuration
of the *Proteftant Faith,* for the *Romifh* : News that I
heard with the moft diftreffing, afflicting, forrowful
fpirit that ever I heard any News. Oh ! I pitty
you, I mourn over you day and night ! Oh I pitty
your weaknefs, that thro' the craftinefs of man you
are turned from the Simplicity of the Gofpel ; I per-
vade my felf you have done it through ignorance.
Oh ! why have you neglected to ask a Fathers Ad-
E   vice

vice in an affair of so great importance as the change of Religion ! God knows that the *Catechism* in which I Instructed you, is according to the Word of God ; and so will be found in the Day of Judgment. Oh ! consider and bethink your self what you have done ! And whether you ask me or not, my poor Child, I cannot but Pray for you, that you may be recovered out of the Snare you are taken in. Read the *Bible, Pray in Secret* ; make CHRIST'S *Righteousness your only* Plea *before* GOD, for *Justification* : Beware of all Immorality, and of Prophaning God's **Sabbaths.** Let a Father Advice be ask'd for the future, in all things of weight and moment. *What is a man profited if he gain the whole World, and lose his own Soul ? Or what shall a man give in exchange for his Soul?* I desire to be humbled under the Mighty hand of God thus afflicting of me. I would not do as you have done for Ten thousand Worlds. My heart akes within me, but will yet wait upon the Lord ; to Him will I commit your case day and night : He can perform all things for me and mine ; and can yet again recover you from your fall. He is a *God forgiving iniquity, transgression and sin : to the Lord our God belong forgivenesses though we have rebelled.* I charge you not to be instrumental to ensnare your poor Brother *Warham,* or any other, and so add Sin to Sin. Accept of my Love, and dont forsake a Fathers advice who above all things desires that your Soul may be Saved in the day of the Lord.

WHat I mournfully Wrote, I followed with my poor Cryes to God in Heaven to make effectual, to cause in him a confideration of what he had done. God faw what a Proud heart I had, & what need I had to be fo anfwered *out of the Whirlwind*, that I might be humbled before Him. Not having any anfwer to my Letter for fome Weeks. I Wrote the following Letter, as I was enabled of God, and fent to him by a faithful hand ; which by the blefling of God was made effectual for his good, and the good of others, who had fall'n to *Popery* ; and for the eftablifhing and ftrengthening of others to refift the Effays of the Adverfary to Truth. God brought good out of this evil, and made what was defigned to promote their intereft, an occafion of fhame to them.

Son Samuel,

I Have waited till now for an anfwer from you, hoping to hear from you, why you made an Abjuration of the *Proteftant Faith*, for the *Romifh*. But fince you continue to neglect to Write to me about it, as you neglected to take any advice or counfel from a Father, when you did it. I cannot forbear Writing again, and making fome reflections on the Letter you Wrote me laft, about the two Women. It feems to me from thofe words of *Abigail Turbet*'s in your Letter, or rather of Mr. *Meriel*, which you tranfcribed for him. [*Abigail Turbet* fent for Mr. *Meriel*, fhe committed her Soul into his hand, and was ready to do whatfoever he pleafed,]

I say, it seems rational to believe, that she had not the use of her reason; its an expression to be abhorred by all who have any true sense of Religion. Was Mr. *Meriel* a God, a Christ? could he bear to hear such Words and not reject them; replying, don't commit your Soul into my hands, but see that you commit your Soul into the Hands of GOD thro' *Christ Jesus*, and do whatever God Commands you in His *Holy Word*. As for me, I am a creature, and can't Save your Soul, but will tell you of *Acts* 4. 12. *Neither is there Salvation in any other; for there is no other Name under Heaven given among men, whereby we must be Saved.* Had he been a faithful *Minister* of JESUS CHRIST he would have said, 'tis an honour due to CHRIST alone. The holy Apostle says, *Now unto him that is able to keep you, and present you faultless before the presence of his Glory, with exceeding joy, to the only wise GOD our Saviour, be glory, and majesty, dominion and power both now and ever, Amen. Jude* 24, 25. verses. As to what you Write about Praying to the *Virgin Mary*, and other Saints, I make this reply, Had Mr. *Meriel* done his duty, he should have said to them, as 1 *Joh.* 2. 1, 2. *If any man sin, we have an Advocate with the Father, JESUS CHRIST the Righteous; and he is the Propitiation for our sins.* The Scriptures say, *There is one God, and one Mediator between God and man, the Man CHRIST JESUS.* Yet CHRIST said, Go and Preach, *He that Believeth, is Baptised, shall be Saved.* The Apostle in *Gal.* 1. Saith, *But though we or an Angel from Heaven Preach any other Gospel unto you, then that we have Preached you, let him be accursed.* They never Preach'd, Pray'd to the *Virgin Mary*, or other *Saints*. As you would be Saved hear what the Apostle saith, *Heb.* 4. 13. &c. *Neither is there any Creature that is not manifest in his sight ; but all things are naked, and opened unto the eyes of him with whom we have to do.* Seeing then that we have a great High Priest that is entred into the Heavens, *JESUS* the Son of God, let us hold fast our Profession : for we have not an High Priest that cannot be touched with the feeling of our infirmities, but was in all points tempted like as we are, yet without sin ; let us therefore come boldly unto the Throne of Grace, that we may obtain Mercy and find Grace to help in time of need. Which words do hold forth, how that CHRIST JESUS is in every respect qualifyed to be a Mediatour and Intercessor, and I am sure they can't be applyed to any meer creature, to make them capable of our Religious trust. When *Roman Catholicks* have said all they can, they are not able to prove, that the Saints in Heaven have a knowledge of what Prayers are directed to them. Some say they know them one way, others say they have the knowledge of them in another way : and that which they have fix'd upon as most probable to them, is, That they know of them from their beholding the face of God ; Seeing God they know these Prayers : But this is a great mistake. Tho' the Saints see and know God in a Glorious manner, yet they have not an infinite knowledge ; and it does no wayes follow, that because they see God, they know all Prayers that are directed to them upon the Earth. And God has no where in His Word told us, that the Saints have such knowledge. Besides, were it a thing possible for

E 2

them

them to have a knowledge of what Prayers are directed to them, it does not follow that they are to be Pray'd to, or have religious honour confer'd upon them. The *Romanists* can neither give one Scripture Precept or Example for Praying to them; but God has provided a *Mediator*, who knows all our Petitions, and is Faithful and Merciful enough, and we have both Scripture Precept & Example, to look to Him as our Mediator and Advocate with the Father. Further it can't be proved that its consistent with the Saints being creatures, as well as with their happiness, to have a knowledge of Prayers from all parts of the World at the same time, from many Millions together about things so vastly differing one from another.: and then to present those Supplications for all that look to them, its not Humility but Will Worship. *Col.* 2. 18. *Let no man beguile you of your reward, in a voluntary humility, worshipping of Angels,* verse 23. *Which things indeed have a shew of Wisdom and Will Worship, and humility.* For what humility can it be, to distrust the Way that God has provided and encouraged us to come to him in, and impose upon God a Way of our own devising? Was not God angry with *Jeroboam,* for imposing upon him after such a sort? 1 *King.* 12. 33. *So he offered upon the Altar which he had made in Bethel, the fifth day of the eighth Month, which he devised of his own heart.* Therefore CHRIST saith, *Mark* 7. 7. *Howbeit, in vain do they worship me, teaching for doctrines the Commandments of men :* Before the coming of Christ, & His entring into Heaven as an Intercessor, *Heb.* 7. 25. *Wherefore he is able to Save them to the utter-*

most

moſt that come to God by him, ſeeing he ever liveth to make interceſſion for them. I ſay before Chriſts entring into Heaven as an Interceſſor, not one word of any Prayer to Saints, what reaſon can be given that now there is of ſo many Saints to make Interceſſion, when CHRIST as a *Prieſt* is entred into Heaven to make Interceſſion for us ? The anſwer that the *Romaniſts* give is a very ſable & falſehood: Namely that there were no Saints in Heaven, till after the Reſurrection and Aſcention of Chriſt, but were reſerved in a place called *Limbus Patrum*, and ſo had not the beatifical Viſion. See *Gen. 5. 24. Enoch walked with God and was not for God took him.* If he was not taken into Heaven, what can be the ſenſe of thoſe Words, *for God took him ?* Again, 2 King. 2. 1. When the Lord would take up *Elijah* into Heaven by a Whirlwind, *verſe 11. There appeared a Chariot of fire and Horſes of Fire, and par ed them both aſunder, and Elijah went up by a whirlwind into Heaven.* Muſt the truth of the Scripture be call'd in queſtion to uphold their Notions ? Beſides, tis not conſiſtent with reaſon to ſuppoſe, that *Enoch and Elias* inſtead of having a peculiar priviledge vouchſafed to them, for their eminency in holineſs, ſhould be leſs happy for ſo long a time then the reſt of the Saints deceaſed, who are glorifyed in Heaven ; which muſt be, if they are yet kept and muſt be till the day of Judgment out of Heaven, and the beatifical Viſion, in an earthly Paradiſe, according to ſome of the *Romaniſts*, or in ſome other place they know not where : according to others. Religious Worſhip is not to be given to the creature, *Mat. 4. 9, 10.* And

And saith, *All these things will I give thee, if thou wilt fall down and worship me.* Then saith *Jesus* to him, *Get thee hence Satan, for it is written thou shalt worship the Lord thy God, and him only shalt thou serve.* That phrase, and *Him only shalt thou serve,* excludes all creatures. *Rev.* 22. 8, 9. *I fell down to worship before the feet of the Angel, which shewed me these things; then saith he to me, see thou do it not, for I am thy fellow servant, and of thy brethren the Prophets, and of them which keep the sayings of this book, worship God.* Which plainly shews, that God only is to be Worshipped with a religious Worship. None can think, that Saint *John* intended to give the highest Divine Worship to the Angel, who saith, Don't fall down & worship me; its Gods due, *Worship God.* So *Act.* 10. 25, 26. *As Peter was coming in, Cornelius met him and fell down at his feet and worshipped him, but Peter took him up, saying stand up, I my self also am a man.* See also *Lev.* 19. 10. The Words of the Second Commandment (which the *Romanists* either leave out, or add to the first Commandment saying, *Thou shalt have no other gods before me,* adding *&c.*) I say the Words of the second Commandment are, *Thou shalt not make to thy self any Graven image, or any likeness of any thing that is in Heaven above, or that is in the earth beneath, or that is in the waters under the earth; thou shalt not bow down thy self to them, nor serve them, for I the Lord thy God am a Jealous God, &c.* These words being inserted in the Letter, that came from your Brother *Eleazar* in *New-England* the last Summer, was the cause of the Letters being sent down from *Mont-Royal,* and not given to you, when so near you : as I suppose

there

there being no other clause of the Letter that could be objected against, and the reason why found at *Queleck*, when I sent it to you a second time enclosed in a Letter Written by my self. The *Brazen Serpent* made by Divine appointment as a Type of CHRIST, when abused to Superstition, was by reforming *Hezekiah* broken in pieces. As to what the *Romanists* plead about the Lawfulness of *Image* and *Saint Worship*, from those likenesses of things made in *Solomons* Temple, its nothing to the purpose. We don't say it is not lawful to make or have a Picture, but those carved Images were not in the Temple to be adored, bowed down to, or worshiped. There is no manner of consequence, that because there were Images made in *Solomons* Temple that were not adored and worshipped, that therefore its now lawful to make and fall down before Images, and Pray to them, and so Worship them. Religious *Worshiping of Saints* can't be defended from, but is forbidden in the Scriptures; and for fear of loosing their Disciples, the *Romanists* keep away from them the Bible, and oblige them to believe as they say they must believe. As tho' there was no use to be made of our reason about our Souls; and yet the *Bereans* were counted noble, for *Searching the Scriptures*, to see whether the things Preach'd by Saint *Paul* were so or no. They dare not allow you liberty to speak with your Father, or others, for fear their Errors should be discovered to you. Again, you Write, "that *Esther Jones* confess'd, that there was an inequality of Power among the Pastors of the Church. An argument to convince the World, that because the
Priests

Priests in fallacious wayes, caused a Woman listempered with a very high Feaver, if not distracted, to say, she confess'd there was an inequality of Power among the Pastors of the Church, therefore all the World are obliged to believe that there is a Pope. An argument to be sent from *Dan* to *Beersheba* every where, where any *English* Captives are, to gain their belief of a *Pope*. Can any rational man think, that CHRIST in the Sixteenth Chapter of *Mathew* gave Saint *Peter* such a Power as the Papists speak of; or that the Disciples so understood CHRIST, when immediately there arose a dispute among them who should be the *Greatest in the Kingdom of Heaven* Math. 18. 1. *At the same time came the Disciples of Jesus, saying, who is the greatest in the Kingdom of Heaven.* The rock spoken of in the Sixteenth of *Mathew*, not the Person of *Peter*, but the confession made by him, and the same Power is given to all the Disciples, you compare one Scripture with another; not one word in any place of Scripture of such *Vicarship* power as of a *Pope*, nor any solid foundation of proof that *Peter* had a greater Authority than the rest of the Apostles. 1 *Cor.* 4. 6. *That you might learn in us, not to think of men above that which is written.* Yea, the Apostle condemns them. 1 C. 1. 12. for their contentions, *One saying, I am Paul, I of Apollos, and I of Cæphas*; no more *Peters* being a foundation than any of the rest. *we are built upon the foundation of the Apostles and Prophets, JESUS CHRIST himself being the chief corner stone.* Not one word in any of *Peters* Epistle showing that he had greater power than the other Apostle

Apostles. Nay if the Scriptures give any preference, it is to Saint *Paul* rather than Saint *Peter*. 1 Cor. 3. 10. *According to the grace of God which is given to me, as a wise Master Builder I have laid the foundation.* 1 Cor. 5. 3, 4. *For I verily as absent in body, but present in spirit, have judged already, as tho' I were present, concerning him that hath so done this deed. In the Name of our Lord Jesus Christ, when ye are gathered together, and my spirit, with the power of our Lord Jesus Christ, &c.* 1 Cor. 7. 1. *Now concerning the things whereof ye wrote to me;* application made not to Saint *Peter*, but *Paul*, for the decision of a Controversy or Scruple. 1 Cor. 11. 2. *Now I praise you brethren, that you remember me in all things, and keep the ordinance as I delivered them to you.* Either those spoken of, *Acts* 15. or in his Ministry and Epistles, 2 Cor. 2. 10. *For your sake forgave I it, in the person of Christ.* 2 Cor. 11. 28. *That which cometh upon me dayly, the care of all the Churches.* 2 Cor. 12. 11, 12. *For in nothing am I behind the very chiefest of the Apostles, though I be nothing. Truly the signs of an Apostle were wrought among you in all patience, in signs and wonders, and mighty deeds;* and in other places. Again if you consult, *Acts* 15. where you have an account of the first Synod or Council, you will find that the counsel or sentence of the Apostle *James* is followed, *ver.* 19. Wherefore *my* sentence is, *&c.* not a word that St. *Peter* was chief. Again, you find *Peter* himself sent forth by the other Apostles, *Acts* 8. 14. *The Apostles sent unto them Peter &* John. When the Church of the Jews found fault with *Peter*, for going in to the Gentiles when he

went

went to *Cornelius*, he does not say, why do you question me, or call me to an account, I am *Christ's Vicar* on Earth. When *Paul* reproved *Peter*, *Gal.* 2. he does not defend himself, by mentioning an infallibility in himself as *Christ's Vicar*, or reprove *Paul* for his boldness.

The Roman Catholick Church can't be a true Church of Christ, in that it makes Laws directly contrary to the Laws and Commands of Christ. As for example, in with-holding the Wine or the Cup from the Laiety, in the *Lords-Supper*; whenas Christ commands the same to drink who were to eat. Their evasion that the Blood is in the Body, and so they partake of both in eating, is a great fallacy built on a false foundation of *Transubstantiation*. For when men eat, they can't be said to drink, which Christ commands, for Christ commands that we *take the Cup and drink*, which is not done in eating; besides the Priests themselves won't be so put off. The words (*this is my Body*) do only intend, this doth signify or represent my Body, which will appear if you compare Scripture with Scripture, for after the Consecration the *Holy Ghost* calls it Bread, and the fruit of the Vine. *Exod.* 12. 11. *It is the Lords Passover*; that is, it represents it. In all the Evangelists, you read of killing and eating the Passover, a few lines or verses before these words, *This is my Body*, which plainly show, that our Saviour in the same way of figurative expression speaks of the *Gospel Sacrament*. If these words were taken as the *Romanists* expound them, he must eat his own Body himself, whole and entire in

his

his own hands ; and after that each one of the Disciples eat him entire, and yet he set at the Table whole, untouched at the same time ; contradictions impossible to be defended by any rational arguments. Yea, his whole Body, must be now in Heaven and in a thousand other places, and in the mouth of every Communicant at the same time, and that both as a broken and unbroken Sacrifice, and be subject to putrefaction. CHRIST is said to be a *Door*, a *true Vine*, a *Way*, a *Rock* ; What work shall we make if we expound these in a literal manner, as the *Romanists* do, when they say, *this is my Body*, is meant of the real Body of Christ in the Eucharist? It's said, 1 Cor. 10. 4. *And did all drink the same spiritual drink : for they drank of that spiritual Rock that followed them : and that Rock was Christ.* Was Christ literally a Rock, think you? Yea, it's absurd to believe, that a Priest uttering a few words over a Wafer not above an inch square, can make it a God, or the Body of Christ entire as it was offered on the Cross. A blasphemy to pretend to a power of making God at their pleasure ; & then eat him, & give him to others to be eaten, or shut him up in their Altars : that they can utter the same words, and make a God or not make a God, according to their intention, and that the people are obliged to believe that it is God, and so adore it, when they never hear any word of consecration, nor know the Priests intention. As to what you write about the *Holy Mass* : I reply, it's wholly an Humane Invention ; not a word of such a Sacrifice in the whole Bible, its being a Sacrifice propitiatory

tiatory daily to be offered, is contrary to the Holy Scriptures. *Heb. 7. 27. Who needeth not daily, as those High-priests, to offer up sacrifice first for his own sins, and then for the peoples : for this he did once, when he offered up himself.* And yet the *Romanists* say, there is need that he be offered up as a Sacrifier to God every day. *Heb. 9. 12. By his own blood he entred in once into the holy place, having obtained eternal redemption for us. 25, 26, 27, 28 Nor yet that he should offer himself often, as the High-priest entereth into the holy place, every year with the blood of others : For then must he often have suffered since the foundation of the world. But now once in the end of the world, hath he appeared to put away sin by the sacrifice of himself. As it is appointed unto men once to die, but after this the Judgment ; So Christ was once offered to bear the sins of many.* Heb. 10. 10. *By which will we are sanctified, through the offering of the Body of Jesus Christ once for all.* ver. 12. *But this man after he had offered one sacrifice for sins, for ever sat down on the Right-hand of God.* ver. 14. *For by one offering he hath perfected for ever them that are sanctified.* By which Scriptures you may see, that the Mass is not of Divine Appointment, but an humane Invention. Their evasion of a bloody and an unbloody Sacrifice, is a flam, the holy Scriptures speak not one word, of Christ being offered as a Sacrifice Propitiatory, after such a sort as they call an unbloody Sacrifice. All the Ceremonies of the Mass are humane inventions, that God never Commanded. As to what in the Letter about Praying for the Women after their Death, is very ridiculous. For *As the tree falls so it lyes ; as Death leaves judgment will find ; no change*

change after Death from an afflicted to an happy place and state. *Purgatory* is a phansy for the enriching the Clergy, and impoverishing the Laiety. The Notion of it a fatal Snare to many Souls, who sin with hopes of easy getting Priestly absolutions at Death, and buying off Torments with their Money. The Soul at Death goes immediately to Judgment, and so to Heaven or Hell. No authentick Place of Scripture, mentions so much as one Word of any such place or state. Mr. *Meriel* told me, if I found one errour in our Religion, it was enough to cause me to disown our whole Religion: by his argument you may see, what reason you have to avoid that Religion that is so full of Errors. Bethink your self and consult the Scriptures, if you can get them (I mean the Bible :) Can you think their Religion is right, when they are afraid to let you have an English Bible ? Or to speak with your Father, or other of your Christian Neighbours, for fear they should give you such Convictions of truth that they can't remove ? Can that Religion be true, that can't bear an Examination from the Scriptures, that are a *Perfect Rule* in matters of Faith ? Or that must be upheld by Ignorance, especially Ignorance of the holy Scriptures ? These things have I written as in my heart I believe. I long for your recovery, and will not cease to Pray for it. I am now a man of a Sorrowful Spirit, and look upon your fall as the most aggravating circumstance of my afflictions, and am perswaded that no pains will be wanting, to prevent me from seeing or speaking with you ; but I know that Gods Grace is all-

sufficient;

sufficient. *He is able to do exceeding abundantly above what I can ask or think.* Don't give way to discouragement as to a return to *New-England*; read over what I have written, and keep it with you if you can; you have no friend on earth that wisheth your Eternal Salvation more heartily than your Father. I long to see & speak with you, but I never forget you; my love to you, and to your Brother and Sister, and to all our Fellow-Prisoners. Let me hear from you as often as you can. I hope God will appear for us before it be long. There are a great many other things in the Letter, that deserve to be refuted, but I shall be too tedious in remarking of them all at once. Yet would not pass over that passage in the Letter, that *Esther Jones* confessed, that there were *Seven Sacraments.* To which I answer, That some of the most Learned of the *Romish* Religion, confessed (without the distracting pains of a violent Feaver) and left it upon record in Print, that it can't be convincingly made out from the Scripture, that there are Seven Sacraments, and that their most incontestable proof is from tradition, and by their traditions they might have found Seventeen as well as Seven: considering that four Popes successively, spent their lives in purging and correcting old Authors. But no man can out of the Holy Scriptures, prove any more than two Sacraments of Divine Institution, under the New Testament, namely, *Baptism* and the *Lords-Supper.* If you make the Scriptures a perfect rule of faith as you ought to do, you can't believe as the Romish

mish Church believes. Oh! see that you Sanctify the Lord Himself in your heart, and make Him
your fear and your dread. *Fear not them that can
kill the body, and after that have no more that they can
do ; but rather fear him that has power to destroy Soul
and Body in Hell fire.* The Lord have Mercy upon
you, and shew you Mercy for the Worthiness and
Righteousness sake of *Jesus Christ,* our Great and
Glorious Redeemer and Advocate, who makes In-
tercession for Transgressours. My Prayers are daily to God for you, for your Brother and Sister, yea
for all my Children, and fellow Prisoners. I am
your Afflicted and Sorrowful Father,

John Williams.

Chateauriche, March 22.
     1706.

GOD who is gloriously *Free and Rich in His
Grace to vile Sinners,* was pleased to bless poor &
weak means for the recovery of my Child so taken,
and gave me to see, that He did not *Say to the House
of Jacob, Seek you me in vain.* Oh! that every Rea-
der would in every difficulty make Him their Refuge ; He is an hopeful stay. To alleviate my
Sorrow, I received the following Letter in answer
to mine.

     ' *Mont-Royal, May* 12. 1706,

' *Honoured Father,*
I Received your Letter which you sent by ------
   ' which good Letter I thank you for ; and for
the good Counsel which you gave me ; I desire to
              F   ' be

' be thankful for it, and hope it will be for the good
' of my Soul.   I may fay as in the *Pfalms* ; *The for-*
' *rows of Death compaffed me, and the pains of Hell gat*
' *hold on me : I found trouble and forrow, then called I*
' *upon the Name of the Lord : O Lord I befeech thee deliver*
' *my Soul ! Gracious is the Lord and Righteous, yea our*
' *God is merciful.*   As for what you ask me about my
' making an Abjuration of the *Proteftant Faith* for the
' *Romifh,* I durft not Write fo plain to you as I
' would, but hope to fee and difcourfe with you.
' I am forry for the Sin I have committed in chang-
' ing of Religion, for which I am greatly to blame.
' You may know that Mr. *Meriel* the School-mafter,
' and others, were continually at me about it ; at
' laft I gave over to it : for which I am very forry.
' As for that Letter you had from me, it was a Let-
' ter I tranfcribed for Mr. *Meriel*: And for what he
' faith about *Abigail Turbet,* and *Efther Jones,* no bo-
' dy heard them but he, as I underftand.   I defire
' your Prayers to God for me, to deliver me from
' my Sins.   Oh remember me in your Prayers ! I
' am your Dutiful Son, ready to take your Counfel.
                                        ' *Samuel Williams.*

THis Prieft Mr. *Meriel,* has brought many Letters to him and bid him Write them over and
fend them, and fo he has done for many others.
By this as alfo by Mrs. *Stilfons,* faying, She does not
think that either of thefe Women did change their
Religion before their Death ; fhe affirms alfo, that
oftentimes during their Sicknefs, whilft they had
the ufe of their reafon, they protefted againft the
                                        Romifh

Romiſh Religion and Faith. Its evident that theſe Women never dyed *Papiſts*, but that it was a wily Stratagem of the Prieſts to advance their Religion ; for Letters were ſent immediately, after their death, to uſe this as a perſwaſive argument to gain others. But God in His Providence gave in farther Conviction of their fallaciouſneſs in this matter.

For the laſt Summer, one *Biggilow* of *Marlborough*, a Captive at *Mont-Royal*, was very Sick in the *Hoſpital*, and in the judgment of all with a Sickneſs to Death. Then the Prieſts and others gave out, that he was turned to be of their Religion, and taken into their communion: But contrary to their expectation he was brought back from the gates of Death, and would comply with none of their rites ; ſaying, that whilſt he had the uſe of his reaſon, he never ſpake any thing in favour of their Religion. And that he never diſown'd the *Proteſtant Faith*, nor would he now. So that they were ſilenced and put to ſhame. There is no reaſon to think that theſe two Women were any more *Papiſts* than he ; but they are Dead and cannot ſpeak. One of the Witneſſes ſpoken of in the fore-mentioned Letter, told me, ſhe knew of no ſuch thing, and ſaid Mr. *Meriel* told her, that he never heard a more fervent and affectionate Prayer, than one which *Eſther Jones* made a little before her Death. I am verily perſwaded, that he calls that Prayer to God ſo full of affection and confeſſion, the confeſſion made by her of the Sins of her whole Life. Theſe two Women always in their health, and ſo in their Sickneſs, oppoſed all *Popiſh* Principles, as all that knew them can teſtify.

so long as they could be permitted to go and speak with them. One of these Women was taken from the *Eastward*, and the other, namely *Esther Jones* from *Northampton*.

In the beginning of *March* 1706. Mr. *Sheldon* came again to *Canada*, with Letters from His Excellency our GOVERNOUR, at which time I was a few days at *Quebeck*. And when I was there, One Night about Ten a Clock, there was an *Earthquake*, that made a report like a Cannon, and made the Houses to tremble : It was heard and felt many Leagues, all along the Island of *St. Laurence*, and other places. When Mr. *Sheldon* came the second time, the Adversaries did what they could to retard the time of our return, to gain time to seduce our Young Ones to *Popery*. Such were sent away who were judged ungainable, and most of the Younger sort still kept. Some still flattered with Promises of reward ; and great Essayes to get others Married among them. One debauched, and then in Twenty-four Hours of time Published, taken into their Communion & Married ; but the poor Soul has had time since to lament her Sin & Folly, with a bitter cry ; and asks your Prayers, that God of His Sovereign Grace would yet bring out of the horrible Pit, she has thrown her self into. Her Name was *Rachael Storer* of *Wells*.

In *April*, one *Zebediah Williams* of our Town dyed : he was a very hopeful and pious young man who carried himself so in his Captivity, as to edify

several

several of the *Eng'ish* ; and recover one fallen to *Popery*, taken the last War ; tho' some were enraged against him on these accounts ; yet even the *French* where he Sojourned, and with whom he Conversed, would say he was a good man : One that was very Prayerful to God, and Studious and Painful in reading the holy Scriptures. A man of a good understanding, a desirable Conversation : in the beginning of his last Sickness he made me a Visit (before he went to the Hospital at *Quebeck*) to my great satisfaction, and our mutual consolation and comfort in our Captivity. As he had several times before, living not above two Miles from me over the River, at the Island of St. *Laurence*, about Six Weeks or Two Months. After his Death, the *French* told me, *Zebediah* was gone to Hell, and Damned : For, said they, He has appeared since his Death (to one *Joseph Egerly*, an *English* man, who was taken the last War) in flaming fire, telling him, he was Damned for refusing to imbrace the Romish Religion, when such pains were used to bring him to the true Faith, and for being instrumental to draw him away from the *Romish Communion*, forsaking the Mass ; and was therefore now come to advertise him of his danger. I told them, *I Judged it to be a Popish Lye* : Saying, *I bless God our Religion needs no lies to uphold, maintain, and establish it, as theirs did.* But they affirmed it to be true, telling me, how God approved of their Religion, and Witnessed miraculously against ours. But I still told them, I was perswaded his Soul was in Heaven, and that these reports were only devised fables to seduce Souls.

For

For several Weeks they affirmed it, telling me, that all who came over the River from the Island affirmed it to be a truth. I beg'd of God to blast this Hellish Defign of theirs, so that in the iffue it might be to render their Religion more abominable, and that they might not gain one Soul by such a ftratagem. After some weeks had paffed in such affertions, there came one into my Landlords House, affirming it to be a truth reported of *Zebediah*, saying, *Jofeps Egerly* had been over the River, & told one of our Neighbours this Story. After a few hours I saw that Neighbour, and askt him whether he had seen *Egerly* lately : he faid yes, What News told he to you ? None faid he. Then I told him what was affirmed as a truth ; he anfwered, *Egerly* faid nothing like this to him, and he was perfwaded he would have told him, if there had been any truth in it. About a week after this, came one *Joſs Boult* from the Island of St. *Laurence*, a Lad taken from *Newfoundland*, a very ferious fober Lad of about Seventeen years of Age ; he had often before came over with *Zebediah* to vifit me. At his coming in, he much lamented the lofs of *Zebediah*, and told me, that for feveral weeks they had told him the fame Story, affirming it to be a truth, and that *Egerly* was fo awakened by it, as to go again to Mafs every day, urging him ; fince God in fuch a miraculous way offered fuch conviction of the truth of their Religion, and the falfhood & danger of ours, to come over to their Religion, or elfe his damnation would be dreadfully aggravated. He (faid he) would have no reft for them day and night ; but (fa

(said he) I told them their Religion was contrary
to the *Word of God*, and therefore I would not embrace it; & that I did not believe what they said.
And says he, to me, one day I was sitting in the house,
and *Egerly* came in, and I spake to him before the
whole Family (in the *French* Tongue, for he could
not speak much *English*) and askt him of this Story,
he answered, *it's a great falshood*, saying, *he never appeared to me, nor have I ever reported any such thing to
any body; and that he had never been at the M ss since
Zebediah's death*. At the hearing of which they
were silenced and put to shame; we blessed God
together, for discovering their wickedness, and disappointing them in what they aimed at, & pray'd
to God to deliver us and all the Captives from de-
lusions, and recover them who had fallen, and so
parted. After which I took my Pen and wrote a
Letter to one Mr. *Samuel Hill*, an *English* Captive,
taken from *Wells*, who liv'd at *Quebeck*, & his Brother *Ebenezer Hill* to make a discovery of this lying
Plot, to warn them of their danger, and assure
them of the falshood of this report; but the Letter
fell into the hands of the Priests, and was never
delivered. This *Egerly* came home with us, so
that they gained nothing but shame by this stratagem: God often disappoints the crafty devices of
wicked men.

In the latter end of Summer, they told me they
had News from *New-England*, by one who had been
a Captive at *Boston*, who said that the Ministers at
Boston had told the *French* Captives, that the Pro-
testant Religion was the only true Religion; and

that as a confirmation of it, they would raise a dead person to life before their eyes for their conviction ; and that having perswaded one to feign himself dead, they came and pray'd over him, and then commanded him in the *Name of Christ* (whose Religion they kept pure) to arise, they call'd and commanded, but he never arose ; so that instead of raising the Dead, they killed the Living ; which the bereav'd Relations discovered.   I told them, It was an old Lye and Calumny against *Luther* and *Calvin* new vamped, and that they only change the persons and place : but they affirmed it to be a truth ; I told them I wondred they were so fond of a faith propagated, and then maintain'd by lying words.

We were always out of hopes of being returned before Winter, the season proving so cold in the latter end of *September*, and were praying to God to prepare our hearts, with all holy submission to his Holy Will, to Glorify his Holy Name In a way of passive Obedience in the Winter.   For my own part, I was informed by several who came from the City, that the Lord *Intendant* said, if *More* returned and brought word that *Battis* was in Prison, he would put me into Prison, and lay me in Irons. They would not permit me to go into the City, saying, I always did harm when I came to the City, and if at any time I was at the City, they would perswade the Governour to send me back again.

In the beginning of last *June*, the Superior of the Priests came to the Parish where I was, and told

told me, he faw I wanted my Friend Captain *de Beauville*, and that I was ragged. But fays he, your obftinacy againft our Religion difcourages from providing better Cloaths; I told him it was better going in a ragged Coat, than with a ragged Confcience.

In the beginning of laft *June*, went out an Army of Five Hundred *Maqua's* and *Indians*, with an intention to have fallen on fome *Englifh* Towns down *Connecticut* River, but lighting on a *Scalacrok Indian*, who ran away in the night, they were difcouraged; faying, he would alarm the whole Country: about Fifty as fome fay, or Eighty as others, returned: Thus God reftrained their Wrath.

When they were promifing themfelves another Winter, to draw away the *Englifh* to Popery, came News of an *Englifh* Briganteen a coming, and that the Honourable Capt. *Samuel Appleton* Efqr. was coming Ambaffador, to fetch off the Captives, and Capt. *John Bonner* with him. I cannot tell you how, the Clergy and others laboured to ftop many of the Prifoners, to fome Liberty, to fome Mony, and yearly Penfions were offered, if they would ftay. Some they urged to tarry at leaft till the Spring of the year, telling them it was fo late in the year, they would be loft by Shipwrack if they went now; fome younger ones they told, if they went home they would be Damned and burn in Hell for ever, to affright them; day and night they were urging of them to ftay. And I was threatned to be fent aboard, without a permiffion to come afhoar again, if I fhould again difcourfe with any of the *Englifh* who

who were turned to their Religion; at *Mont-Royal* especially all crafty endeavours were used to stay the *English*. They told my Child, *if he would stay, he should have an honourable Pension from the King every year, and that his Master, who was an old man, and the richest in* Canada, *would give him a great deal; telling him if he returned he would be poor, for* (said they) *your Father is poor, has lost all his Estate, it was all burnt.* But he would not be prevailed with to stay; and others were also in like manner urged to stay, but God graciously brake the snare and brought them out.   They endeavoured in the Fall of the year, to have prevailed with my Son to have gone to *France*, when they saw he would not come to their Communion any more. One Woman belonging to the *Eastern* parts, who had by their perswasions, Married an *English* Captive taken the last War, came away with her Husband, which made them say, they were sorry they ever perswaded her to turn to their Religion, and then to Marry. For instead of advancing their Cause by it, they had weakened it, for now they had not only lost her, but another they thought they had made sure of. Another Woman belonging to the *Eastward*, who had been flattered to their Religion, to whom a Bible was denied, till she promised to embrace their Religion, and then had the promise of it for a little time, opening her Bible whilst in the Church and present, at Mass, she read the fourth Chapter of *Deuteronomy*, & received such conviction whilst reading, that before her first communion she fell off from them, and could never be prevailed with any more to be of their Religion.

We

We have reason to bless God, who has wrought deliverance for so many, and yet to pray to God for a door of escape, to be opened for the great number yet behind, not much short of an Hundred, many of which are Children, and of these not a few among the Salvages, and having lost the *English* Tongue, will be lost and turn Salvages in a little time, unless something extraordinary prevent.

The Vessel that came for us, in its Voyage to *Canada* struck on a Bar of Sands, and there lay in very great hazard for four Tides, and yet they saw reason to bless God for striking there; for had they got over that Bar, they should at midnight in a Storm of Snow have run upon a terrible ledge of Rocks.

We came away from *Quebeck*, *October* Twenty five, and by contrary Winds and a great Storm, we were retarded, and then driven back nigh the City, and had a great deliverance from Shipwrack, the Vessel striking twice on a Rock in that Storm. But thro' God's goodness we all arrived in safety at *Boston*, *November* Twenty one, the number of Captives Fifty seven, two of which were my Children. I have yet a Daughter of Ten years of Age, and many Neighbours, whose Case bespeaks your compassion, and prayers to God to gather them, being *Out-casts ready to perish.*

At our arrival at *Boston*, we found the Kindnesses of the Lord in a wonderful manner, in God's opening the hearts of many, to bless God with us and for us, wonderfully to give for our supplies in our needy state. We are under obligations to praise
God

God, for difpofing the hearts of fo many to fo great Charity, and under great bonds to pray for a bleffing on the *Heads, Hearts* and *Families* of them, who fo liberally and plentifully gave for our relief. It's certain, that the Charity of the whole Country of *Canada,* though moved with the doctrine of merit, does not come up to the Charity of *Bofton* alone, where notions of merit are rejected; but acts of Charity performed out of a right Chriftian Spirit, from a Spirit of thankfulnefs to God, out of Obedience to Gods Command, and unfeigned Love and Charity to them that are of the fame *Family and Houfbold of Faith.* The Lord grant, that all who devife fuch liberal things, may find the accomplifhment of the promifes made by God, in their own perfons and theirs after them, from Generation to Generation.

———————————————

I Shall Annex a fhort account, of the troubles beginning to arife at *Canada.* On *May* Sixteen, arrived a Cannoe at *Quebeck,* that brought Letters from *Miffyppi,* written the *May* preceeding, giving an account that the Plague was there, and that One hundred & Fifty *French* in a very little time had dyed of it; & that the Salvages called the *Lezilouways* were very turbulent, & had with their Arrows wounded a *Jefuit* in Five places, and killed a *French-man* that waited on him. In *July* News came, that the Nations up the River were engaged in a War one againft the other, and that the *French* living fo among them, and Trading with them,

were

were in great danger, that the *Mitchel-macquina's* had made War with the *Mezianmies*, and had killed a *Mendicant Fryar*, and three other *Frenchmen*, and eleven Salvages at a place call'd the *Straits*, where they are settling a Garison and Place for Traffick ; *the Mitchel-macquina's* had taken sixteen *French-men* Prisoners, and burnt their Trading Houses. These tidings made the *French* very full of perplexing troubles ; but the *Jesuits* are endeavouring to pacify them, but the troubles when we came away, were rather encreasing then lessening ; for the last Letters from the *French* Prisoners at *Mitchel-macquina* report, that the Salvages had sent out two Companies, one of an Hundred and Fifty, another of an Hundred and Sixty, against the Salvages at the *Straits*, and they feared, they would engage as well against the *French* as the *Indians*

The END.

Reports of Divine Kindneſs:

OR,

Remarkable Mercies

Should be Faithfully Publiſhed,

For the Praiſe of

GOD

the Giver.

Set forth in a *SERMON* Preached at
Boſton Lecture, *Decemb.* 5. 1706.

By John Williams,

Paſtor of the Church of CHRIST in *Deerfield*;
Soon after his Return from a doleful Captivity.

Pſal. 107. 13, 14, 15, 22. *He ſaved them out of their diſtreſ-
ſes. He brought them out of darkneſs, and the ſhadow
of death: and brake their bands in ſunder. O that men
would praiſe the Lord for his goodneſs; and for his wonderful works to the Children of men. --- Let them exalt
him alſo in the Congregation of the People, and Praiſe
him in the Aſſembly of the Elders.*
Pſal. 34. 3. *O magnifie the Lord with me, and let us
exalt his Name together.*

Boſton: Printed for S. Phillips, at the Brick Shop. 1707.

Signal Favours to be Publish'd, For the Praise of God the Giver.

Luke VIII. 39.

Return to thine own House, and shew how great things God hath done unto thee. ----

THE Infinitely Wise disposer of all things, who aims at His own Glory, in the Governing of Rational Creatures, doth sometimes bring Persons into the depths of distress, and then magnify his Power & Grace in raising them up out of their afflictions : and in many respects by such things, He has a design of advancing His own Honour & Glory in the World. We find in the context, a Person in a very doleful distress'd condition : he seems to be forsaken of God, and made a Possession and dwelling Place of Evil Spirits, deprived of all humane comforts & delights, made to possess Sorrow and Pain to such a degree, & to be a common Subject, or Theme of discourse for all men to relate doleful things about. And afterward, God in very remarkable & wonderful works of Power and Mercy, not only gives release from his sorrowful Possession, but he is *Sitting at the feet of Jesus, cloathed, & in his right mind.* Now this was done for the declarative and manifestative Glory & Honour of God. For when this man for whom such great things

things had been done, Petitions Chrift that he may abide with Him, to hear from Him, and Pay his refpects to him ; he receives commandment, to be glorifying the Power & Mercy of God, in declaring to others what great things God had done for him.

1. A Subject of great Mercy ; or a perfon fpoken of for whom God had done great things, beftowed eminent Mercies.

2. A particular and fpecial command from Chrift, to be glorifying God in relating to others, what Mercies he had been the Subject of.

3. His obedience to the great command of Chrift; he went and publifhed the great things done for him by Chrift ; fo that from the command of Chrift, & his obedience to it, for which he is commended, you may obferve this Doctrinal Conclufion.

DOCT. *It well becomes thofe who have had eminent Mercies, to be fhewing to others what Great things GOD has done for them.*

The holy Scriptures in many places confirm this Truth. See Exod. 12. 25, 26, 27. *And it fhall come to pafs, when ye be come to the land, which the Lord will give you, according as he hath promifed, that ye fhall keep this fervice. And it fhall come to pafs, when your Children fhall fay unto you, What mean you by this fervice? That ye fhall fay, It is the facrifice of the Lords Paffover, who paffed over the Houfes of the Children of Ifrael in Egypt, when he fmote the Egyptians, & delivered our houfes. Exod. 13. 8, 10. And thou fhalt fhew thy fon in that day, faying, This is done becaufe of that which the Lord did unto me, when I came forth out of Egypt. Thou shalt therefore keep this Ordinance in his season from year to year.* Psal. 78. 3, 4. *Which we have heard and known, and our Fathers have told us; we will not hide them from their Children, shewing to the Generation to come the Praises of the Lord, and his Strength, & his wonderful works that he hath done.* In the prosecution & handling of this Truth, Consider,

1. They who have had Mercies, have had them from God. God is the bestower and giver of all our good things: All our Mercies come to us by a Divine Providence, and ordering; not by casualty and accident: neither are they of our own procuring and purchasing, or others, so as to exclude the providential disposing of God. 'Tis God who returns the Captivity of Zion, Psal. 126. begin. *When the Lord turned again the Captivity of Zion, we were like them that dream: Then was our mouth filled with laughter, and our tongue with singing. Then said they among the Heathen, the Lord hath done great things for them. The Lord hath done great things for us; whereof we are glad: turn again our Captivity O Lord.* The very Heathen, acknowledge the good things bestowed upon, and done for the Church, to be from God; and Gods own People acknowledge Him for the Mercies granted, and humbly supplicate Mercies from Him for the future. 'Tis God who gathers the out-casts of *Israel:* 'tis He who takes away the Captives of the Mighty, the Prey of the terrible; Who contends with them that contend with us, & saves our Children. 'Tis God who disperseth and gathers again: Therefore the Psalmist, Psal. 103. begin. Calls upon his Soul to bless the Lord, and

G

and not to forget all his benefits; and faith, 'tis God *who forgiveth all thy iniquities, who healeth all thy diseases: Who redeemeth thy life from destruction, who crowneth thee with loving kindness and tender mercies,* &c. Sometimes, God in a more immediate and extraordinary way and manner, confers blessings and mercies, sometimes in a more ordinary and mediate way; but his Providence is to be acknowledged in all: not one single Mercy comes to us, without a commission from that God by whom our very Hairs are numbred.

2. It well becomes those who have had eminent Mercies, to be showing to others what great things God hath done for them. Therefore you find the holy Psalmist calling upon others, to give a listning ear, whilst he makes a Narration of the Salvations he had from God, Psal. 66. 16. *Come and hear all you that fear God, and I will declare what he hath done for my Soul.*

1st. *Reason.* Because God aimed at the advancement of His Own Honour and Glory, in the giving and dealing out of these Mercies. God makes and disposeth all things for His own Honour and Glory. All Works of Providence, are some way or other to advance the Honour & Glory of God in the World. The glory of His Power, Wisdom, Mercy, Justice and Holiness, are some way or other advanced in a declarative and manifestative way and manner. Now it well becomes us, to fall in with the design of God, and in an active manner to be giving His Glory. That God designs to have Glory given Him, is evident from. Psal. 50. 15. *And call upon in the day of trouble, I will deliver thee, and thou shalt glorify me.* Exod. 7. 5. *And the Egyptians shall know that I am the Lord, when I stretch forth mine hand upon Egypt, and bring out the Children of Israel from among them.* God has a design to magnify His Power, Mercy and Covenant Faithfulness, in the eyes of the World.

2d. *Reaf.* Because God has given us direct precepts, and positive Commands, in this Way to be Glorifying of Him. *God is our Lord and Law-giver,* and He requires that among other ways of shewing forth His Praises, we do it by rehearsing His Praise worthy Acts, to the Children of Men. So that in Obedience to God, and answering that High & Noble end we were made for; its requisite that in this way we glorify God. Its enough, that the great God who hath taken us into *Covenant Relation* to Himself, has enjoyned us, to shew forth His Praises in rehearsing to others the Salvations, and Favours we have been the Subjects of. The fore-mentioned Scriptures, with many others that might be enumerated, sufficiently demonstrate, that God calls for our thankful acknowledgments in this Way; and upon the account of this being so agreeable to the revealed and preceptive Will of God, the Psalmist expresseth himself, as in Pfal. 145. 4, 5, 6. *One Generation shall praise thy works to another, and shall declare thy mighty acts. I will speak of the glorious honour of thy Majesty; and of thy wondrous works. And men shall speak of the might of thy terrible acts: and I will declare thy greatness. They shall abundantly utter the memory of thy great goodness: and shall sing of thy Righteous-*

ousness. Verse 10, 11, 12. *All thy works shall praise thee, O Lord: and thy Saints shall bless thee. They shall speak of the glory of thy kingdom, and talk of thy power. To make known to the sons of men his mighty acts: and the glorious majesty of his kingdom.*

3d. *Reas.* Because hereby they will stir up others to bless God with them, and for them. A truly gracious Soul finds by experience, that he can do but a little in Glorifying God, finds how far he falls short of the rule of duty, in so reasonable a Service as Glorifying God. And being enlarged in desires that the glory due to God might be given Him, doth call upon others to joyn with him in this Heavenly Service of Praising God; and therefore tells them what great things God has done. *Psal.* 34. 2, 3, 4, 6. *My soul shall make her boast in the Lord: the humble shall hear thereof, and be glad. O magnify the Lord with me, and let us exalt his Name together. I sought the Lord, and he heard me; and delivered me from all my fears. This poor man cryed, and the Lord heard him; and saved him out of all his troubles.* When *Moses* told his Father in law *Jethro*, the great things God had done for *Israel*, he Glorifies God on their behalf, *Exod.* 18. 8. *&c. And Moses told his Father in law, all that the Lord had done unto Pharaoh, and to the Egyptians for Israels sake, and all the travel that had come upon them by the way, and how the Lord delivered them. And Jethro rejoyced for all the goodness which the Lord had done to Israel: whom he had delivered out of the hand of the Egyptians. And Jethro said, Blessed be the Lord, who hath delivered you out of the hand of the Egyptians, and out of the hand of Pharaoh, who hath* *delivered the people from under the hand of the Egypti-* *ans. Now I know that the Lord is greater than all gods;* *for in the thing wherein they dealt proudly, he was above* *them.* By this means thanks will be given to God by many : as many have been Praying to God for them, so many will be praising and blessing God with them and for them.

4*th. Reaf.* Because hereby they will oftentimes be advised and counselled, how to improve such Mercies to the Glory of God. We are conscious to our selves of so much blindness, ignorance, and darkness, that we can't but own it a great thing to be in a way for the best counsel, what to do with our Mercies, and what and how to return to God for them. Now the publishing the great things done by God for us, put others in a capacity to be advising and telling of us, what temptations we may expect to meet with, and what will be needful on our part to avoid temptations, and how to over-come ; they will be counselling us, how to be in a way, of rendring to the Lord according to the benefits done unto us : what Duties God looks for the performance of, and directions how to do duty. In a word, we may be counsel'd how to order our whole Conversation, so as God may have Glory, and our good purposes of honouring and glorifying God with our Mercies, established. *Prov.* 20. 18. *Every purpose is established by counsel.* When *Moses* had told *Jethro* what great things God had done for Israel, he saith, Exod. 18. 19. *Hearken now* *unto my voice, I will give thee counsel, and God shall be* *with thee.* &c.

5th. Reas. Because hereby they will be instrumental to put others upon trusting God, making Him their hope and refuge in an Evil Day. Others will be excited, to a seeking refuge under the shadow of his Wings, Psal. 44. beg. *We have heard with our ears, O God, our fathers have told us, what work thou didst in their days, in the times of old. How thou didst drive out the Heathen, &c.* And then it is said, *Thou art my King, O God: command deliverances for Jacob. Thro' thee will we push down our enemies: through thy Name will we tread them under that rise up against us. For I will not trust in my bow, neither shall my sword save me. In God we boast all the day long.* Others that have heard, will say, such and such an one was thus exercised, and God appeared for them, and put songs of praise to the Lord into their mouths, we will commit our Case to God too; we will both hope and quietly wait for Gods Salvation too. Your telling others, how you have found God a Prayer-hearing God, will encourage them, Prayer-wise to be committing their distressed & difficult cases to Him. What an honour to be instrumental to any Souls comfort, and Gods honour; agreeable to this is that, Psal. 78. 5, 6, 7. *Which he commanded our fathers: that they should make them known to their Children. That the Generation to come might know them, even the Children which should be born: who should arise and declare them to their Children: That they might set their hope in God, and not forget the works of God: but keep his Commandments.*

6th. Reas. Because the Works of God towards them, have been very wonderful. The Psalmist often

speaks

speaks of the Works of God as marvellous; they are wonderful if we confider, how God *Tim'd* the Mercy; when their feet well nigh flipt, when they could fee no way of efcape; as with the Children of *Ifrael* at the Red-fea. How very wonderful and marvellous was the work of God, in putting by the wicked purpofe of *Haman* againft *Mordecai* and the Jews? If we confider how God kept from fal-ling, by making them pafs a right judgment on their ways and His ways, as *Pfal.* 73. Yea appearing to fave them, when with *Jonah* they were faying, *They were caft out of Gods fight.* All refuge feemed to fail, none fhewing any care for their foul; even then God made good his word on which he had caufed them to hope, as *Pf. l. 142. per totum.* The Works of God are marvellous, if we confider the way and manner of ufhering in the mercy, the inftruments that were made ufe of, and how He difappointed the counfels of the Crafty.

7th. Reaf. Becaufe 'tis a good evidence, that they regarded and took notice of the Works of God in Mercy, and would not forget His wonderful works towards them. For hereby, they put others under advantages to put them in mind, what favours they have received from God.

USE. I. Of INSTRUCTION.
And,
Firft, It informs us, that its very acceptable to God, for Chriftians to entertain the report of the experiences of others, to excite their own hearts to glorify God. For if God make it a duty in the
receiver

receiver to report, it layes the hearer under an obligation, to set such remarks upon the passages of Divine Providence to others, as may be useful to engage their hearts to Glorify God, for the favours and blessings He has bestowed upon others. And therefore In obedience to Gods Command, that you may be under advantages to Glorify God; I will now make a report, of some of the great things God has done for those, you have been putting up so many Prayers to God for. God has eminently been fulfilling that Word, *Psal.* 106. 46. *He made them also to be pitied, of all those that carried them Captives.*

God hath made such whose Characters have been, that they were such whose tender Mercies were Cruelties; such from whom, one act of pity and compassion could scarce be expected, even such who have delighted in cruelty; to pity & compassionate such who were led into Captivity by them. Made them bear on their Arms, and carry on their Shoulders our *Little Ones,* unable to Travel. Feed their Prisoners with the best of their Provision: Yea, sometimes pinch themselves, as to their daily food, rather than their Captives. To pity them under Sickness, and afford all proper means for the restoration of their Health, or recovery from Lameness. Made Heathens bowels earn towards poor Infants expos'd to Death, so as to Work out their deliverance from fatal strokes, by burdening of themselves. Oh! let us adore the riches of the Grace of God, *who in wrath remembers Mercy, and doth not stir up all His wrath*; and from hence be encouraged, when under convictions of Gods being

angry

'angry with us, yet lock to Him for Mercy.

God has upheld many poor Souls under all manner of difadvantages, as to a getting of Knowledge, and kept them from falling, though crafty Adverfaries were under all advantages, and painful endeavours to feduce them. Being without *Bibles*, *Minifters*, or *Chriftian Friends* to confer with, daily harrafed with Temptations, and Tempters : Some threatned, fome flattered, fome fhut up and confined in Monafteryes, where no means were uneffayed to gain them to change their Religion.

God has ftrengthened to go through tedious Journeys, and renewed ftrength, when they were even fainting in their Spirits : thinking it not poffible to Travel Five Miles, and yet enabled to Travel at leaft Forty in a day. Remarkably ordering feafons, fo as to be for their comfort in their Travels ; caufing a Moift Snow, to fall on the Lake, only to fuch a height as to make it eafy to their Swoln and Wounded feet : Changing the Winds for their advantages, in petty Voyages in their ticklifh Cannoes.

They have found God a little Sanctuary to them, in the Land of Strangers ; even there have found the Confolations of God through Chrift not to be fmall ; fo that fome of the moft joyful and refrefhing favours from Heaven, have been given in to their Souls, when under all forts of outward afflictions.

. They have found God a God hearing Prayers, when they have gone to Him with their moft difficult cafes, preferving them from falling ; recovering theirs from falls ; to a making void the counfels

of

of Adverfaries, difappointing of them in the things they dealt moft Proudly in. God has brought His to a refignation to His Will, and then appeared dealing out Mercies, as the very cafe did require.

God has Sanctified to fome, their former *Sabbath* folemn attendances on Duties of Piety, Private as well as Publick ; and a Religious Education to be an unanfwerable Objection, againft fuch who were zealous for the *Traditions of Men,* to a vifible Prophaning Gods Sabbaths. They durft not embrace that Religion whofe Principles as well as Practifes, were fo contrary to the Precepts of Gods holy Word. Oh ! how fhould *Minifters,* and *Parents* be encouraged from hence to ufe their utmoft care, that Gods Sabbaths may be duely Sanctified by all under their charge ; and that they would be exemplary before others, in a due obfervance of Holy Time.

God has made the falls of fome to *Popery,* a means for the recovery of others ; and making thofe things, by which the adverfary thought to encreafe their numbers and profelytes, to be occafional of recovering fuch who from their youth had been educated in the *Popifh* way ; having been taken Captives when young. Don't be difcouraged and fay, your Friends and Relations have (being Captivated when young) for a long time lived in *Popery,* and therefore no hopes of recovery ; for God can make dry bones, very dry to live, and can in ways unthought of by you, both recover them after they have fallen, and return them again. The Adverfaries have fometimes, pretended miracles for the confirmation of their Religion, that

they

they might feduce to Popery ; in fallacious ways caufed reports that fome Captives dyed *Papifts* ; that one appeared in *Flames of Fire* to bear a teftimony againft the *Proteftant Religion ;* but God has in his wife Providence, made known their falfhoods and lyes.

They have fought to perfwade fome, by Sums of Mony to change their Religion, offering honour and advancement to them at the fame time ; but God has enabled to refift and hate fuch allurements.

The reading the fourth Chapter of *Deuteronomy,* a means of recovering one from *Popery.*

God has made fome with an heroical, yea with a right Chriftian Courage to welcome Death. Oh let every one get fuch a preparednefs for DEATH, that a fudden DEATH may not be a terror !

God has made fome by the want of Sanctuary Mercies, to fet an higher value upon the Ordinances of JESUS CHRIST. Oh learn to prize and improve them, left God teach you by the briars and thorns of the Wildernefs, the worth of them, and weep when you fet down at the Rivers of *Babylon.*

God has ftrengthened fome to ftand, when they have not only been threatned with all cruelties if they refufed, but when the Hatchet has been lift up, with a threatning of fpeedy death in cafe of refufal. Oh let every one truft in God, who is a feafonable help and a prefent refuge !

I N 4.

INSTRUCTION, II.

How they are to blame, that do not regard and take notice of the Works of God, nor treasure up the remembrance of them in their minds. How soon are mercies like to be forgotten; the Pfalmist fays, *Forget not all his Benefits.* It was the great fin of the *Ifraelites* of old, that they foon forgat Gods wondrous works. The Holy God gave order, that his People fhould Erect Stones of remembrance, that his Wonderful Works of Mercy to his People might not be forgotten; yea, commanded Parents to tell their Children, from Generation to Generation, what great things he had done for them. How are they then to blame that fay, *They blefs God for their Mercies,* and don't rehearfe the Praife-worthy Works of Divine Providence to others.

USE II.

To direct fuch, who have received great and eminent Mercies from God, in this way of making known to others the wonders of mercy to them, to be praifing God. It's one way very proper and agreeable to the revealed Will of God: You muft watch againft all vain Oftentation,

USE III. OF EXHORTATION.

To all who have in a more peculiar way and manner, been cafting off the effects and fruits of

Divine,

Divine Bounty and Goodnefs, to be declaring what great things God has done for them,

Therefore,

1. Beware of all manner of Pride. Sometimes men can't declare the Great Works of God done for them, without making known their own weaknefs, and therefore are filent, and hold their peace; they had rather God fhould lofe his Glory, then they any of their credit or efteem. But the holy Pfalmift fays, *His feet had well nigh flipt; yea, that in his hafte he had faid, all men are liars;* and that one day he fhould furely perifh: takes fhame to himfelf, that he might magnify the preventing and delivering grace and goodnefs of God. Sometimes mens *Pride* makes them fo admire their own parts and contrivances, as to overlook the Works of Divine Providence; they *facrifice to their own net, and burn incenfe to their own drag;* and fay they had fo much *Learning & Knowledge,* that they could eafily anfwer arguments to feduce them to *Popery;* and fo don't fee and acknowledge the goodnefs of God, in preferving and keeping of them.

2. Beware of a *ftupid, fenfelefs,* flothful Spirit. *The works of God are fought out of them that have pleafure in them.* Some won't be at the pains to recollect the paffages of Divine Providence; won't commit them to writing, or to their memories, and therefore foon forget them; they never wifely obferve the heightning circumftances of their Mercies.

Confider,

Confider, 3. How Heavenly an Employ & Serv[ice] it is, to be Glorifying and Praifing God. It w[ill] be one part of the work of Heaven, to be telli[ng] of the wonderful Works of God towards us. [Be]gin fuch an Heavenly Employ on Earth. Here[by] you will alfo intereft your felves in the *Prayers* [of] others ; to have many Prayers going daily t[o] God for you, how great a favour is it! Othe[rs] hearing what Mercies you have had, will bear yo[u] upon their hearts when at a Throne of Grace, that you may fuitably improve fuch mercies.

The Glorifying God. is the greateft and chiefe[ft] concern of gracious Souls ; and the Glorifying [of] God here, is the way to be Glorifyed by, an[d] with God for ever. The notGlorifying God is ver[y] difpleafing to Him, and a way to deprive our felves of the fweet and comfort of our Mercies. God accounts forgetting of *Mercies*, a forgetting Himfelf.

FINIS.

Printed in the United States
16930LVS00001B/51